MW00465015

Rhee Kun Hoo was born in 1935, during imperial Japan's occupation of Korea. Rhee worked as a psychiatrist and taught at Ewha Womans University during his fifty-year career, making indispensable contributions in the field of mental health care in South Korea, where he is considered a visionary. He was the first to introduce an open-ward system and psychodrama as a therapy method in psychiatric facilities in the country, and also served as the president of KNPA (Korean Neuropsychiatric Association). After retirement, Rhee and his wife have dedicated themselves to providing postwar Korean generations with guidance in life such as parenting, counseling, relationship advice, and postretirement life coaching. Rhee has written over ten books in Korean to date, including his bestselling debut essay collection, *I Want to Have Fun Till the Day I Die* (Galleon, 2013), which has sold around 800,000 copies in Korea.

Suphil Lee Park (Translator) is a bilingual poet, translator, and writer born and raised in South Korea before finding a home in the States, where she studied English Literature and Poetry at NYU and the University of Texas at Austin. She wrote the poetry collection *Present Tense Complex*, winner of the Marystina Santiestevan Prize (Conduit Books & Ephemera, 2021), and a forthcoming poetry chapbook, *Still Life*, selected by Ilya Kaminsky as the winner of the Tomaž Šalamun Prize. She also won the Indiana Review Fiction Prize and received a fiction prize from *Writer's Digest*. Her translations of Korean literature have appeared or are forthcoming in the *Cincinnati Review*, the *Los Angeles Review*, and *New England Review*, among others. Her own work can be found in the *Iowa Review*, the *Kenyon Review*, and *Poetry*, among others. Find out more about her at: https://suphil-lee-park.com/.

If You Live to 100,
You Might as
Well Be Happy

If You Live to 100, You Might as Well Be Happy

Essays on Ordinary Joy

RHEE KUN HOO

Translated from Korean by Suphil Lee Park

UNION
SQUARE
&CO.

NEW YORK

**UNION
SQUARE
& CO.**

NEW YORK

UNION SQUARE & CO. and the distinctive Union Square & Co. logo are
trademarks of Sterling Publishing Co., Inc.

Union Square & Co., LLC, is a subsidiary of Sterling Publishing Co., Inc.

Text © 2019 by 메이븐 (Maven)
Illustrations © 2024 Younggeun Byun
English translation copyright © 2023 Suphil Lee Park

All rights reserved. No part of this publication may be reproduced, stored in a
retrieval system, or transmitted in any form or by any means (including electronic,
mechanical, photocopying, recording, or otherwise) without prior written permission
from the publisher.

First published in Korea by 메이븐 (Maven, Korea) in 2019. This translation first
published in Great Britain in 2024 by Rider, a division of the Penguin Random
House group of companies.

ISBN 978-1-4549-5442-2
ISBN 978-1-4549-5443-9 (e-book)

For information about custom editions, special sales, and premium purchases, please
contact specialsales@unionsquareandco.com.

Printed in the United States of America

2   4   6   8   10   9   7   5   3   1

unionsquareandco.com

Cover and interior illustrations by Younggeun Byun

Contents

Contents

PROLOGUE

THIS YEAR, I TURNED eighty-seven. Now anyone can take one look at me and tell I'm elderly. When I walk, I take laborious, slow steps, as if time's on my side; I'm hunched over and my hair is unmistakably white.

Eight years ago, I slipped while walking downstairs and hit my head. Upon falling, I thought that was the end for me. I thankfully recovered after a month of hospitalization. Still, since then, I've felt the always-looming death even closer than before.

Montaigne wrote that being acquainted with death will liberate one, but I still find the thought of death unfamiliar and terrifying.[1] It's just that now I understand death to be an unavoidable part of my life, and I live the best I can, trying to find some morsel of peace with this unchangeable fate. Every morning, I envision, eyes closed, what to do that day and whom to meet. And while I busy myself flitting from one task to the next all day long, thoughts about death quiet down and leave me alone for the time being. How grateful I am for those moments of peace.

Since my accident, I've been slowly losing sight even in the one good eye I have left. In old age, I've always relied on the computer to stay connected to the world: listening to online lectures, participating in virtual community activities, and talking with friends. But now I can't even use the computer on my own.

With a pile of commissioned manuscripts to work on, I turned to my grandchildren. I asked them to help me continue to write by dictation, and they gladly took on the task as a sort of part-time job. The time I got to spend with my grandchildren has helped me deal with the grief that comes with my partial blindness. You see, the loss of health may be agonizing, but when you decide to insert "even so" in this circumstance, when you really try, there is still a bright side or two. As an old Korean saying goes, "You learn to use gums in place of teeth" (이가 없으면 잇몸으로 산다).

When I was a young man, I believed hard work and a strong will could make most dreams come true. After nearly a century, however, I now know that our world is unreasonable and absurd. Not many things can be achieved by hard work alone, and nothing will survive the test of time. Hence, you could say life is a sad affair. It's a process of learning all the weaknesses of your very being.

But in all this, there's a silver lining. This grief that comes with life can also be healed by its smallest pleasures. The canonical Korean writer and activist Shin Young Bok once said, "Even when you're wallowing in devastating grief that compels you to bury yourself on the spot, life's profound mystery remains that such grief can often be soothed by the littlest of pleasures you can imagine. A gulf of grief doesn't need joy of the same scale to be endured and overcome."[2]

Not that I would dare compare myself with this great Korean writer who spent twenty years of his youth in prison, but I essentially feel the same way. The unforeseen joy of every day lived to the fullest helps drown out the feelings of loss and helplessness that sweep over me in the face of all those years behind. So I say, one must *choose* to live happily. Life doesn't fall apart as long as you keep these little moments of joy and laughter nearby. Those moments are always within reach.

Since I published my debut nonfiction book in South Korea back in 2013, I have had a lot of opportunities to connect with my readers. Many readers were intrigued by my success story of becoming a bestselling writer in my seventies, postretirement, and eager to get some personal insights into the ethos of my work: having fun and aging well. So one of the questions I most often get is, "How come you managed to have so much fun?" And my answer is always the same: "When did I ever say I *had* fun? I said I *want to* have fun."

Reader, my life hasn't exactly been plain sailing. I broke my back working day and night in my youth just to make ends meet, and was forced to handle crises when I found myself in prison, and then later in the army, with four kids to raise. As a psychiatrist, I spent most of my adult life trying to improve the conditions of South Korea's fledgling mental health system, facing small and big challenges along the way. All in all, mine was an ordinary life, with repetitive days and life's curveballs alternating in turn. Now, in old age, I'm battling seven different health conditions, so how much fun could I possibly have?

But I've always tried to find some fun in whatever situation I'm in, and make a game out of it. I might not have had a fun life in any traditional sense, but it has been one doggedly in search of happiness.

Some readers have asked me how I could manage to commit myself for such a long time to not one, but a number of missions—volunteer work, studies, hiking, and writing—without burning out. The thing is, I wasn't really planning to. If I had, I wouldn't have lasted long. I was just going to have fun doing all these things, for as long as I wanted, and that, ironically, was key to not burning out. Great pleasure ungained becomes great disappointment. But ordinary joy is easy to find, and an accumulation of little joys can eventually become great happiness.

For over fifty years, treating mental health patients as a psychiatrist and teaching medical students at college, I've always explored this question—what causes us so much emotional, psychological suffering? In my experience, there are two major causes. One is regret about the past, the other is anxiety about the future. Both are inevitable, of course, but both need to be tempered. The past cannot be changed, regardless of your regret, and the future cannot be avoided, regardless of your anxiety. What's worse, these two will keep eating away at the joy you can find, right now, in your life in the present.

If you find yourself turning in bed anxious and full of regret some nights, consider it a sign that you need to accept your life as is. Regrettable or satisfying, it is your life, your own. What can be done now about the mistakes that you've already made? Have you not tried your best, after all? It's time to give yourself some well-deserved pats on the back and tell yourself that you've done well, that it's all good. No matter how prepared you might think you are, you cannot escape the inevitable process of aging and loss ahead. Yes, it's important to prepare for what awaits, but if you cannot learn to ease your nervous mind, you'll miss out on the joy you can find in your present.

Not knowing begets fear, and knowledge makes you brave. It holds true for the big picture of life. The more you come to understand about life, the more prepared you become for whatever life has in store for you. If you're going through that phase of learning right now, I hope my book will be of some help. And in retrospect, you might also realize, as I did, that you have lived your life by some specific rules of your own, that patterns have emerged from the way you have lived.

This is of course just my personal story, and I'm not here to overgeneralize. My wish is for this book to become a starting place for you, my reader, to discover your own life's guiding principles. Because those rules you accrue across your whole life, unique to each of us, are the best tools you have to navigate life's challenges—tools you've been forging all this time without knowing.

PART 1

THE HARD TRUTH ABOUT GETTING OLDER

1

No One Likes Getting Old

WE MORE OR LESS divide life into five stages: infancy, adolescence, young adulthood, middle age, and old age. Each transition to the next stage results in anxiety and pain due to the inevitable uncertainty. And so we've come up with what we call rites of passage for these stages. To announce the change in your role and come to terms with the anxiety you experience in the process. In the past, eighteenth birthdays, weddings, and funerals were the primary rites of passage, but today, admission to college or first significant employment might have become important rites of passage as well.

Let's take a moment, however, to consider if we have any rite of passage for the elderly. Because I can't really think of one. Back in the day, Koreans deemed the sixtieth birthday a special day and made a big deal of it, but now we skip right to the seventieth birthday, which also tends to be a pretty quiet, low-key event even when we do celebrate. All these changes make it complicated to decide what age we should consider "old" now. You see, the concept of old age itself has evolved over time, leading to a bit of cognitive dissonance on my part.

There was a senior professor I always looked up to and was quite close with. Once retired, he frequented the university hospital where I worked for regular checkups. One day, I heard a ruckus coming from the admissions desk in the hospital. At first I brushed it off, thinking it was just a small problem with a disgruntled patient, but when it escalated to yelling I hurried out of my office. To my disbelief, I found my retired senior professor hollering at a receptionist. I ushered him into my office and asked him what had happened. It turned out that he felt the member of staff, who didn't recognize him at all, failed to show him enough respect.

"I'm an emeritus professor here . . ."

Of course, once you retire from teaching and leave the school, there will be fewer and fewer people who recognize you. Every few years, each school becomes an entirely different scene, full of new students, so who would remember an emeritus professor, regardless of honor or esteem? Not to mention that he wasn't even on the medical school faculty but belonged to an entirely different department—who could really fault the staff?

My senior professor must have been going through a tough time accepting his changed role and place in the world. I was taken aback by the unexpected behavior of a respected scholar I also deeply admired as a human being. Was this not undeniable evidence of the challenges that transitioning to old age poses us, seeing the toll it takes even on such a great person? That very day, with my own retirement not too far ahead, I decided to practice living as an old man named Rhee Kun Hoo—who'll be stripped of his titles as professor and doctor. It was an aging training of sorts.

I chose the subway as my place for practice. First of all, subway riders were complete strangers so I wouldn't mind all that much what they thought of me. And because of our Korean culture of giving up one's seat for the elderly, I would be able to accurately tell how old people thought I was. On the subway train, I avoided the seats designated for the elderly and intentionally stood near the regular seats. It wasn't during rush hour, so only a few people had failed to secure seats and were standing. I took a look around and could tell I was probably the oldest person on the train. A young man was sitting right in front of me, and I was curious if he'd stand up and ask me to take his seat, as is customary. But for several stops, he didn't budge. And he even shut his eyes as if to avoid my gaze, which made me feel an odd sense of challenge: Well, let's see how long you last!

I'll be honest with you, reader, I usually never even thought of getting near those seats reserved for elderly and disabled people on Korean subways. I always considered them spots for those who truly needed them. And never did I feel entitled to subway seats at all times just because of my old age, without any truly hindering physical issues or handicaps, and god knows I thought the same when it came to people offering their seats to me—or the elderly in general for that matter. But, good grief, once I decided to see how I'd be treated as a senior citizen out in the world, this young man's behavior started to irritate me. I stood in front of the young man, my eyes shooting daggers, all the way to my destination.

It was a shocking first experiment, but I couldn't form my opinion based on one isolated experience, so I got on another train. This time, a high school student sprang to his feet right away.

"Grandpa, please take my seat."

And this time, I was shocked again. What, Grandpa? And I found myself just as upset as I was with that young man who didn't offer me his seat. I awkwardly told the high schooler, "I'm getting off at the next stop, so I'm good."

And then I hurriedly got off at the next stop, which wasn't even my destination. I murmured to myself: "What a hypocrite! I want to be treated like an elder, but hate being called Grandpa, huh!"

Before that day, I'd always considered myself a laid-back person who couldn't care less about age, hierarchy, or authority. Wasn't I always the nonauthoritarian father, friendly senior student, and unassuming doctor? And yet here I was, getting upset over these complete strangers whom I thought weren't treating me appropriately for my age. I felt my cheeks burning hot with shame at this naked truth. I was no different from a teenage boy who claims all his rights but avoids his responsibilities—I wanted all the respect for my old age, but didn't want to be treated like an old man. What double standards! From that day on, I've worked on myself to change this mindset. First of all, Grandpa was by all means a perfectly valid designation for me now, with my retirement just around the corner. In South Korea, it's customary for men past a certain age to be referred to by this respectful and friendly term. People in South Korea typically address each other—especially in formal relationships—by their professional titles or age groups. To those younger than me, naturally, I'd be Grandpa, if not Doctor. Still, I must have been resisting it somehow. But resistant or not, I wasn't going to stop my aging process or find myself miraculously rejuvenated overnight. It was all a matter of acceptance now. And not accepting my age was always going to be my loss and no one else's. Because, after all, if I don't learn to accept my old age, I'll always be offended when someone calls me Grandpa.

Through such detours, I came to recognize my old age and own it. Fortunately, now, with much practice under my belt, I smile when young people ask me to take their seats on the subway. I remember to thank them. And if they don't offer me a seat, I no longer feel anger, either. I just assume they must be exhausted. This is the precious peace I've gained after the crucial rite of passage for the aging: accepting my age.

Many people in my social circle appear to have experienced these so-called psychological measles, for better or worse. Remember, reader, it is perfectly normal to feel upset in this contradictory way—to not want to feel old and yet, at the same time, to want to be treated with respect for your age. If you one day find yourself battling this contradictory feeling, don't beat yourself up. Instead, consider it a rite of passage. After this rite of passage awaits a peaceful life, I promise.

The American political columnist Michael Kinsley, at the young age of forty-two, was diagnosed with Parkinson's and had to experience aging at a much faster pace than most people. Through this time of drastic change, he poured his heart out in a book, *Old Age: A Beginner's Guide*. In the book, Kinsley describes how he went for a quick swim every morning before heading to work, and one morning, he ran into an old man. The man chuckled at Kinsley and confessed, "I am ninety years old!"

Kinsley replied, "Wow, you don't look your age!"

His ego boosted and chest all puffed up, the man proclaimed: "I used to be a judge!"

Kinsley wrote how, after this, the judge's facial expression seemed to betray a realization of just how absurdly irrelevant this statement was. How he seemed to realize that he had overplayed his hand. He had left this stranger in the pool thinking the very thought he had wanted to dispel: The old fool is past it.

Every one of us, I believe, has had an embarrassing moment like this. Of course, I'm no exception. When I was young, I dreaded the long stories my senior professors told, always starting with "Back in the day," but look at me today—I'm not so different, after all! I've always tried to keep myself in check in the company of my junior professors and younger colleagues. Now, imagine a social gathering of retirees—it's quite the pageant! Our conversation revolves around our past glories. Why so? I'll tell you, my reader, we want to fluff up our lesser present. There's an old saying that was popular among

Korean refugees from the North during the Korean War: "In the north, I used to have a golden calf in tow everywhere I went!" (이북에 살 때는 금송아지 메고 살았어). All this bragging, of course, was a way of licking their wounds in times of diminished means.

The popular Korean song "The World Is a Wonderful World" by Shin Shin Ae reflected on the fairness of life with lyrics about winners going on winning in life while losers continue to lose. But truth be told, winners have it easy, while losers don't. So-called losers would naturally have a hard time accepting their own inferiority. The late, pioneering psychologist Alfred Adler recognized inferiority as a motivation for improving upon one's dissatisfying present. So it's not always a bad thing to encounter some losses. But in a worst-case scenario, it might become an inferiority complex—leading to despair over our helplessness, lack of motivation, or self-deception as a way of hiding our inferior traits and attempting to feel superior to others.

Capitalism, unsurprisingly, capitalizes on feelings of inferiority and insecurities. When I was still teaching, a door-to-door salesperson once visited my office selling encyclopedias. This salesperson tried to pressure me into buying them, arguing that a scholar, any respectable scholar at that, *needed* this series of British encyclopedias. But I wasn't convinced I'd be able to finish the whole collection, and, if it came to that, I could always borrow them from a library. I declined and told him that I had no money on me. This salesperson, instead of backing off, suggested that he could introduce me to a great loan program if I wanted him to. But I kept shaking my head, and there it came, an ace up his sleeve.

"Professor, professor! You really should feel ashamed that you don't own these!"

Yes, this guy was playing on my sense of inferiority. I answered: "Of course, I am deeply ashamed."

The salesperson caved in, and threw his hands in the air. He even explained why he resorted to such an aggressive tactic near the end. He had a manual on how to manipulate people into buying the encyclopedias when they wouldn't budge, and the very last tactic on that manual was an attack on the potential buyer's sense of pride. What if I'd had enough cash on me that day? I think I might have taken the bait, and later regretted the purchase. Indeed, inferiority is a powerful emotion.

In old age, beware your feelings of inferiority. A lot of things don't go your way as you age. First of all, the glorious health of your youth is no more. With less stamina, you naturally become more vulnerable to depressive feelings. Your financial means and social influence will also be on the decline. This is true especially in a society like South Korea that is so concerned with labels. Your alma mater, educational history, official and corporate titles—these labels all serve as ways to differentiate people, to establish a hierarchy. So it's understandable that retirees who have experienced greater past glories often find it even harder to accept their new realities, without these labels to help define them. That's probably why some of them even get new business cards listing all of their past titles. In short, they want to advertise that their humble present doesn't represent their glorious past.

It's not like I don't see where they're coming from. I do. It is hard to embrace life as it is, with all that changes in the passing of time. Yes, we all understand we must, but our hearts still find it hard to take. But refusing to accept your new reality won't do you any good, and a feeling of inferiority can lead to overreactions. You might demand VIP treatment everywhere, just because of your past titles, end up lecturing younger generations when it's not welcome, or curse the world out of spite, like an old grump. Some people spend a fortune on plastic surgery to morph themselves back to how they looked in youth, or become obsessed with taking excessive amounts of supplements and using hardcore gym equipment—all to the chagrin of everyone around them.

But you see, aging is not a fate anyone can escape. We will all eventually end up past our prime. Just as all forms of life must come to an end, we humans also walk the path of decline after our biological and social primes. And once it happens, bragging about your past will not change your present. Even if you wallow in tortuous feelings of inferiority, you can't expect great sympathies from all directions. This is the ruthless but natural truth of life. And how foolish—this pointless wrestle with your own past self!

If someone were to ask me about one must-have life skill, without a second thought, I'd answer *jung-gyeon* (정견 / 正見), the ability to see things as they are, to see yourself for who you are. We in our old age need this sense of astute self-awareness. To look the physically diminishing, socially retreating, financially less competitive self, straight in the eye. If you feel anger, accept it and acknowledge that you're angry. Your old age is not your punishment. Your past was glorious, and your present is good as it is. My reader, set yourself free from that self-sabotaging sense of inferiority.

2

LET'S FACE IT, YOU'RE NOT GETTING ANY HEALTHIER

I ONCE VISITED A senior professor of mine who had been hospitalized. He had finished his studies abroad and become a full-time professor in his twenties, a great feat in itself back then. But after retirement, he suffered the onset of dementia and was soon forced to spend his life at home, in someone else's care at all times. When I paid him a visit, and asked him if he recognized me at all, he simply smiled. He couldn't even spell out his own name in Korean. What happened to my brilliant senior professor, who used to teach his students in native-level English? My heart broke for him. What's worse, his wife confessed to me that dementia had affected her gentle husband's temperament and he would act violently, which was so hard to cope with.

As an old man myself now, the two things I fear most are death and the lack of control that comes with illness. But what could fear ever accomplish? There's no foolproof way to ward off all possible diseases, especially with this aging body of mine. What can I really do other than remain vigilant and take good care of my health?

With age, your health goes downhill. Naturally so. Even though you might still have moments of glowing health, they're fleeting and the big picture points to a gradual, consistent decline. There's a medical term called irreversibility—which means, just as you cannot go back in time, there is some damage to bodily functions that you cannot reverse by any means. The human body itself has this nature of irreversibility. It's destined for an inevitable decline and eventually a complete loss of all its functions. And none of us has ever outwitted this fate.

Which is to say, fearing bad health or being in complete denial will only entail more suffering on your part. In old age, your health conditions will only increase in number, not decline. And, listen, when they do, you shouldn't be too hard on yourself for not taking perfect care of your health, because it's a natural course of life. And since your conditions aren't going anywhere—I hate to tell you, my reader—you'd better learn to deal with them.

I have seven different health conditions. Diabetes and high blood pressure are of course chronic conditions that come with my age, but I also suffer from a herniated disc, gout, gallstones, and CAD (coronary artery disease), and I'm blind in my left eye. There's no way to recover my eyesight, but thanks to a series of successful surgeries and regular checkups, I can live comfortably enough even with my herniated disc and CAD. Funnily enough, what really keeps me on edge, of these seven conditions, is diabetes and high blood pressure, since these are chronic conditions that require close attention on a daily basis. At first, I tried to improve my conditions. I restricted my diet, and on days when I overate, I obsessively went out for long walks. When I first got the diagnosis, I was working at Ewha University Hospital, so I'd be all over Jongno District in Seoul every single day, trying to get in those ten thousand steps. But all these efforts were hard to maintain. In the end, I realized I needed to accept these health conditions as my inevitable companions now, instead of seeing them as problems to be solved. So I changed my mindset to focus on keeping them under control instead of trying, in vain, to get rid of them.

Here are the two principles that I've lived by in order to keep my chronic conditions under control. First, I put complete trust in my doctor and follow their instructions faithfully. Even now, I always take my medication as instructed, like clockwork, but refrain from researching too much or interrogating my doctor about them. I only ever bring up new symptoms of discomfort. Just because I have medical knowledge myself doesn't mean I should go overboard with investigating everything having to do with my own health conditions, which, speaking from experience, will only induce stress and anxiety on my part. If I am to live my life with these conditions, I'd better force myself to become compliant and willfully ignorant to some extent. Sometimes that crucial degree of willful ignorance is what gives you the strength and patience to put up with your conditions.

Second, I focus not on doing what's good for my health but on *not doing* what's bad for my health. When I brought up my conditions, many of my acquaintances, eager to help, recommended a number of drugs and holistic measures. I did try out quite a few of them, but the truth is, I can't really attest to their legitimacy. They actually did not do much more than add to my stress by extending my daily to-do list! So I decided, instead of hoping for the best with all these experiments, just to avoid the absolute vices, such as excessive drinking, smoking, and keeping irregular hours. I knew I could keep up with these simple measures that focused on not-doing rather than doing.

So I've lived comfortably with my many health conditions for over thirty years now. The daily measurements I took of my blood pressure and blood sugar now amount to forty notebooks in total. Had my goal been to cure all of my diseases, I would have waved a white flag a long, long time ago. But once I decided not to fight them, or deny reality, I was able to manage them much better. Reader, an old body's bound to have a health condition or two. The reality is that treating one condition, at times, can create another. (The diagnosis of diabetes particularly unnerved me at first; it was a side effect of my herniated disc medications.) So it's better for your mental health that you don't aspire to the impossible goal of perfect health. And remember, having health conditions does not mean unhappiness. Life can still be satisfying if you manage your conditions well enough.

In a few years, I'll likely have more than seven health conditions to deal with. The future in old age is uncertain and uncertainty is frightening. But fearing the future doesn't help us to face it. Fear only begets more fear. It's more productive to accept your health conditions and figure out how to live with them—try to see them as bad-tempered friends. It's even better if you don't try to outwit them at all. Don't get too ambitious with your health goals and instead learn to manage your conditions by following your healthcare routine regularly and consistently. Only then will you find the strength to live with your illness and not let it define your life. This is my best advice for you, having lived with seven health conditions for more than thirty years now.

3

The Reality of Family Ties

ONE DAY, YEARS AGO—when all of my children were living in their own nuclear families—one of my grandsons showed me a drawing he had done at school on the subject of "family." The drawing left me speechless. My grandson had left me and my wife out of the drawing! Even his pets were included over us! It occurred to me that I must feel less a part of the family to my grandson than his pets, and I felt a surge of bitterness.

But then I nodded to myself, understanding. Yes, I was slightly upset, but my grandson drew what he knew to be true. Family as we were, living apart, my grandson must have felt his grandparents didn't fall into the category of *genuine* family. It reminded me of what had happened when my eldest son was in elementary school and had also been asked to draw his family. Apart from himself, he drew his three siblings and me and my wife. But there was something off about his drawing. I—his dad—was just a body, faceless, in his drawing. My son was used to seeing me asleep and buried under the covers on my days off, just my feet sticking out, so he drew what he'd always seen at home. It was an honest drawing.

I now live with my grandchildren, and their drawings have changed. Their honest drawings now include me and my wife. How thankful I am! Meanwhile, we've also expanded our family with new animal companions. The history of my family's adorable pets having grown to be true life companions coincides with the history of me and my wife having become a true family to our grandchildren.

Now that we all live in the same villa, our family has two dogs and a number of cats, counting the strays we take care of. Before we moved in together, we already had a dog, but once our villa was completed, my youngest son's parents-in-law also sent us a Jindo dog as a gesture of celebration. Of course, not everyone in my family was a dog lover, but after a family meeting, we decided to adopt this Jindo dog. But those who were not big fans of dogs remained skeptical.

Then it happened that we had to enroll our dog (who we named Al Dong) in a canine training program. About a week later, we received a phone call from the trainer. We were told that Al Dong wasn't fit for the training program. In short, Al Dong was expelled. We were all dejected and worried. We thought this might have upset Al Dong more than us. But soon, we found out that Al Dong was completely untouched by this incident. He was just happy to see the family again. Even those in my family who opposed his adoption shared in these moments of joy and worry.

Not long after his expulsion, we had an accident with Al Dong. My son-in-law prepared a special treat for Al Dong and fed it to him himself. Trying to unstick the treat from the bottom of the bowl, he tapped it on the floor with loud knocks. Triggered by this gesture and sound, Al Dong bit my son-in-law's hand. Ironically, my grandson—my son-in-law's son—was the one who got furious over this accident. He couldn't accept how Al Dong had dared to bite his dad's hand. My grandson strongly argued that Al Dong must be put down for his wrongdoing. Dear reader, all the effort we made to calm him down would bring tears to your eyes! We—my entire family—tried everything in our power to persuade my grandson. Every one of us was all over him, pleading and begging for forgiveness on behalf of Al Dong. Only after my grandson received a number of gifts and promises of favors was Al Dong forgiven.

Now Al Dong has come to count as a family member, without a shadow of doubt. We feel safe just with the thought of him guarding our house in our absence, and we can no longer imagine going home without Al Dong welcoming us back. We have shared many moments of laughter and tears with him. The same goes for the rest of our family. When we first decided to move in to the villa in the early 2000s, we were often awkward with each other, found family meetings uncomfortable, and felt like strangers at times.

But now we've spent over twenty years together, sharing moments of laughter and tears. Even when we have been fighting and apart, we've soon rushed back to each other and put our heads together with an enemy on the horizon, and have often even asked for forgiveness on behalf of another family member. And through all this, we have become a true family. Now we know how to treat one another, what our triggers are, and we can finish each other's sentences with just one look, all with great respect.

Even though my wife and I are now included with our animal companions in our grandchildren's drawings, the joke's still on me, because I'm not entirely sure where I fall in the ranks of the family. After all, there's a dark joke Koreans make about how grandparents must get in the car before everybody else in the family on a moving day, just so they won't get left behind. But jokes aside, some days when Al Dong welcomes me back home, wagging his tail, I do wonder if I hold a pretty similar place to him in my family.

Reader, you might assume, just as I once did, that being related by blood is all it takes for you to be a family. But in old age, you must realize the reality of family ties and acknowledge that it takes much more—ample time, trial and error, and a lot of shared joy and hardship—for you to come together as a truly supportive, loving family. Remember—families by blood may not always translate into true families. All the time spent together brings us closer, day by day, to *become* a real family. It's the conflicts, misunderstandings, and tears that truly cement family ties.

4

Your Children Become the Parents

"DAD, DRINK A LOT of water!"

Said the email from my eldest daughter, one day last summer when all of South Korea was simmering. On top of the heat-health alerts going off all day long, my wife and I had been getting these constant warnings from our children. Every hour, we would get a phone call or message reminding us to drink a lot of water and remember to get some rest. Of course, we were the ones who had it worst, dealing with the heat, but our children surely went through a lot, worrying about us. So we dutifully kept ourselves hydrated. All of these worried words of my children reminded me that I was an old man now, no doubt.

What's worse, I am, so to speak, a walking general hospital with my various illnesses. So, of course, my children worry. They have done ever since I fell down the stairs and injured my head. When I was finally released from the hospital, thankfully with no serious bone fractures or brain injuries apart from surface wounds, my kids forbade me from going hiking.

What a heartbreaking sentence—I spent most of my life hiking and always found peace in the mountains. For sometime, yes, I'd been denying how weak I'd gotten whenever I went hiking, but now that my children had gone so far as to ban hiking altogether, I was absolutely devastated and had to finally face this harsh truth: I was no longer fit for this passion of my life! But in old age, you're wise to listen to your children, just as in their youth, your children looked up and listened to you. Yes, I know this reversed position might feel a bit humiliating at first, but you have to respect your children's opinion now and sometimes even negotiate with them to reach an agreement more in your favor. I certainly did, because I managed to talk my kids into allowing me to take strolls along the low, well-maintained trails around town—Olle Trail and Dulle Trail.

On a good day, I like to take a taxi to the pavilion in Buam-dong from where I'll stroll back to my house in Gugi-dong. But taking this stroll is also a joy that I'm allowed only once in a while now. Sweltering days, freezing days, rainy days, days of yellow dust all aren't fit for my short trip, and I feel it takes more energy each time to get ready and go out on a simple stroll. Someday, even a stroll will be too much of a risk. I can't begin to imagine the devastation I will feel then, when I find it hard enough to handle this lesser sentence. But what can I do? I'll take as many strolls as I can, when I'm still able to go out and walk along the trail on my own. That certainly is the pleasure I can enjoy right now, and only now.

One of the biggest changes you experience in old age is no doubt of the body. From here on out, your health is only going to get worse. Your eyesight will worsen, so will your hearing, and you will, so easily drained, find going out on your own harder and harder, just as I have. Your memory's not like it was before, so you'll blink on a lot of things, forget important meetings, and have to live with a condition or two.

In your eighties, this aging process escalates even more. I'd spent my life teaching, but sometime after my eightieth birthday, I noticed that delivering a decent lecture required twice as much effort, with my concentration waning. In my youth, the entirety of my lecture just flowed straight from my mind through my mouth, but in my eighties, PowerPoint was my savior more than a few times. It was the only way I could keep myself on track and from forgetting the content altogether. And during a Q&A session at the end of each lecture, I'd walk over to stand near the audience with a question and listen carefully with my eyes closed. In part, it was because of my bad hearing, yes, but it was also because it took all my mind's power to understand the audience clearly and articulate my answer. In my youth, I would have urged the audience to ask question after question, and answered them all at once, with a conclusive and detailed response to all of the major points brought up during the session. But it's all too much now—to summon up all that concentration and logical thinking on the spot! Writing's not the same anymore, either. Since my good eye—my right—has been getting worse for sometime, I can't see what's on the computer screen very well, and even when I manage to decipher something on my own, I need a lot of breaks between glimpses. Writing a single page can now take days.

A while ago, I got my prescribed drugs after a regular checkup, and my wife, who accompanied me, saw the amount and, appalled, said: "How do you fit all those in your stomach?"

But who can escape this curse of aging? All we can do is listen to our doctors, take our prescribed drugs dutifully, and manage our conditions. If your memory's not the same, mark important dates and appointments on your calendar, and if you have a hard time concentrating, why not seek out the help of newfangled equipment and find ways to adapt to your aging body? You can't just sit and wallow because you're not as lithe and healthy as before. Yes, it's a shame that in old age we have to deal with physical and psychological tolls, but it's also a new reality that you'll have to accept sooner rather than later.

Having been a mental healthcare worker my whole life, I've worked with numerous patients. And most of my patients looked much older than their age. Pain—and a lasting one, at that—can do that to you. But it was not only psychological issues that pestered them and changed their looks. My patients also often complained about their physical conditions. And they'd rant about the aches all over, their heavy hearts, and all of the things and people not to their liking. Even though I listened respectfully, listening being an important part of my job, whenever my patients complained about their various physical conditions, I also couldn't help thinking to myself that I would never just give up and complain because things weren't going as I wished and I had challenging physical conditions.

At this age, I finally see in that younger version of myself a young man who found it hard to relate to his ailing patients. I carry this sense of guilt deep inside now, but this too was inevitable. The truth of aging and a weakening body can be wholeheartedly understood only by those who have gone through it themselves. Which is to say, my reader, it's of little use to complain about your physical and psychological pain from aging—the younger generations, however hard they may try, won't truly understand you until they walk miles in your shoes later in life.

How do we remain dignified despite our physical conditions, in old age? By accepting the phenomenon of aging itself, but seeking out and enjoying what we can, while we still can. We Koreans say, tongue in cheek, "Have you been old? I was once young!" But I don't believe this proverb validates the older generation's right to justify themselves. In truth, when older, you've been old and you've been young, so your capacity for acceptance and spectrum of expression must be fuller.

Why whine or complain, when there are more respectable and sophisticated ways to communicate the conditions of your aging? We shouldn't overlook our own dignity even in old age.

"Dad, did you drink some water?"

My daughter would follow up with a phone call, far from satisfied with her emailed reminder. This is one of those moments—my children always worrying about my health, or my junior scholars telling me to "take good care of my health"—when I'm forced to confront how old I am. A little voice in my head says, whenever something like this happens, with a hint of resistance: "I'm perfectly fine! My mind's as good as new!" But I never say this out loud. Because all of them are right, and this little voice is just my sadness about having to accept my aging body and mind. It's time to embrace that sadness, while learning not to resist the advice from my children and acquaintances. And I tell myself, "Yes, I should listen to my children and acquaintances. Why not strive to be a good father?"

Still, some days I feel resentful and grumpy. When I do, I try to talk myself out of a bad mood with this pitiful excuse: "I'm not going on a hike not because of my health, but because my children worry about me too much!" I know it's childish, but this excuse is such a salve to my wounded pride and aching heart. And so comforted, I can continue to refrain from complaining and remain dignified despite all the disadvantages that come with age. I know it doesn't sound like much, but I'm telling you, my reader, it's an effective way to graciously accept your aging self.

5

IT'S TIME TO BECOME
A GREAT LISTENER

As a young man, I always wondered about two things when talking to the elderly. One was why they said so many things of no substance, and the other was why their voices were so loud. They'd often end up rambling once they got started, and I'd feel the conversation went nowhere or dragged on too long. I'd even feel embarrassed for them when they didn't read the room right. Yes, again and again, I found myself saddened to see my senior professors, once known for their prized wisdom and concise and logical insights, lose their train of thought in their older years. Some of them even wouldn't let go of the microphone in a public place of discussion like a scholarly conference. Occasionally, they would outright ignore the moderator's attempt to steer the conversation, persisting in airing their thoughts. More than once, I vowed to myself that I wouldn't become like that in old age. But you know what? Now that I'm their age, I think those senior professors must have thought the same when they were younger, too.

"Dad . . ."

This is how the warning of my children usually begins, three fingers raised to remind me that I've repeated myself three times. Yes, I said *warning*, exaggerated though it may sound. And this warning makes me flinch every single time. I'd think, "I don't remember having said this so many times!" Sometimes I suspect that my children fib out of disinterest, but most of the time they must be right. So I have got into the habit of starting every conversation with "As I've said before . . ."

Sometimes, though, I do feel it's necessary to share my perspective on life and values with my children. And I try my best to dilute my advice with a touch of humor to avoid sounding like an overbearing parent. Even so, my children sometimes respond with "Dad, please take it down a notch," to my embarrassment. And I'd be reminded of my senior professors and how I must come across just like they did in their later years. Sometimes my children even tell me: "Dad, please don't bicker with Mum so much!"

I'd say, "What do you mean? When did we get into a fight?"

"You did. I heard you guys yelling . . ."

This misunderstanding usually comes from the volume of our conversation having undoubtedly dialed up in our old age. I find the elderly often raise their voices to accommodate the listener, but we're also unable to accurately gauge the volume of our own voices because of hearing loss. Now that my wife and I are elderly, our loud conversation might have sounded like arguing to my young daughter. I couldn't help laughing at myself, an unmistakable mirror image of those senior professors I was so determined not to take after.

Allow me to defend ourselves, my reader, as a validated representative of the elderly. Why do we talk so much? Well, I've found in old age I have a harder time focusing on one thing now. A conversation is meant to serve a purpose. And in order to serve that purpose well, you add flesh to the spine of your conversation. Let's say a conversation is a tree—that makes the core of what you want to say the trunk of your conversation, and all the detours and fillers the branches. But since we can, in older age, have trouble focusing our mind on one thing, we miss causal links too easily and take too much of a leap in our associative thinking. A lot of branches without the trunk, so to speak. As the Korean saying goes, we start off well but we end up in Samcheonpo. By the time we realize we're off track, we usually don't even remember what we were trying to say, the conversation already completely derailed.

I've found that it's also because of experience. The older you are, the more experiences you're bound to have, and the more convinced you become of your values and perspective on life. In short, we—the elderly—have a lot to say. Believe me, our hearts are in the right place—we just want to help, guide, or share in your joy. Yes, we might want to teach you some lessons on life we deem valuable.

But does an elder's teaching have much relevance for young people today? Back in the day, we respected our elders for their wisdom. So they said the death of an elder was comparable to the closure of a library. But that was at a time when you gained knowledge mostly through firsthand experience. Young people these days, however, have an immense amount of information at their fingertips that they effortlessly navigate on a day-to-day basis. They interpret various languages with a few clicks on their smartphones and consume video content from all around the world. The sheer amount of information easily available to us now is such that some even sarcastically say we've become "trash cans for data." In a world like this, no matter how hard-earned or precious, your experience might not be so relevant or rare anymore.

I used to email my grandchildren stories of my childhood. It was my sincere effort to communicate with them. Even though my grandchildren loved my tales that sounded as if they were straight out of a storybook, they were also equally bewildered by the choices I'd made or how I'd generally reacted in a given situation. They usually expressed their bewilderment in one of the following three ways:

"Grandpa, that's stupid."

"Grandpa, you're so naive."

"Grandpa, I have no idea what you mean."

Kids are now far more educated and worldly than they were in my day, so I expected the first two. But I was at a loss for words when it came to the third reaction. They had no idea, not because my writing was too obscure, but because the ways of my thinking were just so completely different from theirs, and so they didn't understand what I was trying to say at all. In sixty years the world has completely changed. So how would I say my personal experience is of any value to these kids living this vastly different world today?

Some may ask if I mean that once old, we should just keep silent. Well, not quite silent but, yes, in short—talk less and listen more. You need to have something in common with your audience if you want meaningful communication. The more you find in common with your audience, the deeper your conversation can go. And who do you think has a better chance at finding that essential common ground between the elderly and youth? Naturally, it's the elderly, having experienced both past and present. So we need to be the ones to take that first step to understand the youth's perspective. We should listen to them. We may not be able to experience the world as they do, but we should try to understand how different it is for them. If you still can't understand, you should at least admit to that ignorance on your part.

Listening is not a passive, one-sided act at all. The psychological term "abreaction" denotes the process of releasing suppressed emotions and alleviating anxiety by revisiting or reenacting painful experiences lodged in the subconscious.

The simple act of listening well can help your audience achieve this feat of abreaction. So the most important part of a psychiatrist's job is to be a great listener.

Nowadays, things are tough for the younger generations in ways that are very much unlike our times. Not one thing seems to go well for them—school, work, marriage, or child-rearing. They've experienced the extreme competition of our tumultuous modern age, which often proves dehumanizing and harmful to their self-esteem. Despite all their hard work, there will be less security and financial stability for them than there was for us. How crushing is this forecast? Maybe, just maybe, what they need is not a teacher but a listener.

As a little kid, I got along with my grandmother incredibly well. She was a good-natured woman who had a progressive mind for her highly patriarchal time. Even in college, I liked to discuss matters of the world with my grandmother. I admired her for her progressive thoughts and wanted to be like her when I grew older. But when I look back, I realize that the real reason I so enjoyed my conversations with her was because she really listened to me; she always had a benevolent smile on her face and encouraged me to talk, nodding at everything I said, so I kept chattering like a little bird.

I'm not sure when it started, but as I grew older I'd often find the event coordinator approaching me stealthily at post-conference events to whisper: "Professor, you must be exhausted after such a long day."

Of course, a scholarly conference usually goes on for the entire day, so by the evening everyone's tired. But we all look forward to the after-event to chat and catch up with each other, so I definitely didn't want to miss out. Whenever approached by a coordinator like that, I'd first say, "Oh, I'm perfectly fine."

But after a moment, the coordinator would come back to whisper again, "Professor, it's OK if you do feel tired."

Let's say I'd deny it again; that's when a fellow scholar would join the chorus and say, "Oh, it was a long day. You should get some rest."

Then, finally, it'd strike me—I had missed my chance for a graceful exit when the coordinator had asked a second time! Don't get me wrong, dear reader, I'm certain they all sincerely cared about an aged scholar with health conditions. But of course, there's also the undeniable fact that I'm usually one of the most senior professors present, which makes my presence a reason for most people at an after-event to behave. I'd chuckle at myself, recalling how I used to be in my youth.

As a young professor, I used to be entrusted with the task of sending home senior faculty members at after-events. Young academics look forward to the after-event, wanting to relax and have fun among themselves. But having an elder present at the event, especially in a society like South Korea with a hierarchy based on age, makes things rather somber. Even if the elder is perfectly amicable and approachable, everyone feels pressured to behave and speak respectfully. So, assigned with this important mission, I would wait for the right moment and swoop down on the senior professors when they looked even remotely tired: "Sir, aren't you getting tired?"

And they would rub their faces in confusion, wondering if they did feel tired. I wouldn't stop but would take a step further: "Sir, I've called a taxi for you!"

And they would have to get in the taxi and leave the after-event, half willingly and half gently forced. Well, there's a Korean saying: "With youngsters, close your mouth and open your wallet." How cruel! Old age is no crime, but why would the elderly always have to heed the social climate to this extent? But when I look back on my own youth, I certainly see a kernel of truth in that old saying. Still, I cannot help feeling a bit left out. At those after-events I'd often think, "Darn it, I can stay for a bit longer—I wish they'd let me linger just a little more!" But in our later years, as well as knowing how to listen, we should know when to make a graceful exit. Now, the stars of these social events are the next generation. If you try to steal the spotlight now, it might be nothing but *noyok* (노욕), "greed in old age," on your part. The true virtue of the elderly lies in their self-control. In a way, my junior professors were helping me exercise this difficult virtue of self-control, so I should really be grateful.

Of course, self-control is a dignified skill for anyone, young or old, but it's especially important in old age. It's the ability to stop when you should, which requires self-awareness. You need to understand and correctly gauge who you are and what situation you're in, all of which informs you of when it's time to exercise this virtue.

I have a great teacher who taught me about self-control. He was my form tutor when I was in high school, and after the graduation of my class, he went on to teach at a university, where he retired. I had a chance to meet him again at one of our alumni gatherings. We were middle-aged by then, and unanimously agreed to invite him to give a speech. We all missed him—a man way ahead of his time who had an open mind and a big heart to care for every single student of his with genuine interest.

I took charge of inviting him. When I visited him for the first time in a few decades, he welcomed me warmly. I explained what the occasion was and extended the invitation. But my teacher turned it down, point-blank. He expressed that he knew he'd likely ramble on, too excited about reuniting with his students after such a long time. Lately, he felt himself getting long-winded in conversation and going off track too often.

But I wasn't about to give up. I persuaded him, telling him how much everyone had learned from his forward thinking and open-mindedness, and how much we all missed him. But he kept telling me, "I'm not that young teacher you remember anymore, and will only disappoint everyone if you all are expecting that young man I used to be." Finally, I had to put my foot down and plead, "Sir, it's not like we haven't changed ourselves. We're all middle-aged now; we're not those young boys anymore, either!" At this, my teacher finally relented, but on one condition. He was going to jot down a little memo of what he wanted to say in concise words and just read from it, not a word more.

Honestly speaking, a middle-aged man at the time, I didn't fully comprehend why he was so insistent on keeping his speech brief. But when it was time for my teacher to deliver his talk at our reunion, I immediately understood why. The gathering itself kicked off to a great start: a jubilant reunion of students and their beloved teacher. So many memories flooded back, and suddenly everyone looked just like they had decades ago. At the peak of our gathering, it was finally time for my teacher to speak. He took out that memo and started reading. Just like in the old days, his speech was filled with insightful teachings, and each word reflected his progressive thinking. But a few sentences in, he got too excited. He got ahead of himself and off track, losing his usual coherence. Just as he had feared! I quickly wrote a note asking him to wrap up, and when my teacher saw the note, he had a small outburst mid-sentence: "Oh, this is great! This is precisely why I didn't want to come, but boy, did you insist!"

And we all burst into laughter.

All his efforts to keep his speech brief were in vain, but the way he managed the situation left a deep impression on me. Back then, I didn't think much beyond, Oh, what happened to that brilliant, disciplined man? But as I grew old myself, I realized my teacher had shown an admirable degree of self-awareness and self-control, which is, as I've come to learn, incredibly rare.

Really, how many people in their old age manage to be so acutely conscious of their changing behavior, and work so hard on improving themselves? How many can genuinely distinguish what they're capable of from what they're not? I know far more people who seem to view their old age as a title of privilege, acting obnoxiously or trying to drown out everyone else, believing they should be heard before anyone else. But how wise was my teacher? He first considered others and decorum, pondering whether he would be a fitting addition to whatever event or gathering he was invited to.

Remember, your dignity comes from knowing when to stop. We older generations, who were the main characters of society in our prime, now need to step aside and take on supporting roles. You might find it hard to put complete trust in the younger generations, whether they are your junior colleagues or children, but you should realize that it's not in your hands anymore. But this also means you're free to enjoy the rest of your life with the time and energy you will save.

So then, my fellow elders, in our old age I offer you those two pieces of advice: to listen and to know when to excuse yourself. As the first line of the beautiful poem "Falling Blossoms" by Lee Hyeonggi puts it: "How beautiful is the back of the person leaving, knowing when to leave."

PART 2

DON'T LEAVE WITH REGRETS

1

LIFE'S TOO SHORT FOR RAIN CHECKS

I KNOW A PROFESSOR, Kim Jae Eun, who is four years my senior. He's one of the pioneers of educational psychology in South Korea and has dedicated his entire life to its teaching and research. His integrity is unmatched, and he still contributes to society with his academic prowess. Now pushing ninety, he remains a model of mental vigor and positive approach to life, and I couldn't be more proud of him. You might infer from all this respect that I'm some sort of disciple, but no, we are simply close friends who frequently engage in debates. In other words, Professor Kim is open-minded and generous with his friendships.

He likes to say, "Throughout my life, I've always been surrounded by good people!" This is his way of expressing gratitude for having many people in his life who are dedicated to bringing happiness to others. He often emphasizes that in old age, if you miss someone, you should act immediately. Delaying, he warns, might lead to lifelong regret, as he himself experienced.

Professor Kim told me that he was very close with a senior colleague—his former doctor, Park Moon Hee. I also knew Dr. Park from my time at the national psychiatric hospital where he served as the director. Even then, Dr. Park had a significant following due to his pioneering efforts to improve the then-grim conditions of the South Korean mental health system. In a nutshell, he was unparalleled in the field of psychiatric studies. One day, Dr. Park phoned Professor Kim and asked, "Professor Kim, you don't miss me anymore, do you?"

Dr. Park was not a sentimental man. His calls usually concluded with a friendly, nonchalant "Let's grab lunch together sometime." But then, out of nowhere, this unusual question? Professor Kim was momentarily lost for words, but managed to muster a response: "Oh, of course, I'll visit you soon, maybe even next week! I was just thinking about you!"

A week later, Professor Kim learned of Dr. Park's passing. His decision to postpone their meeting by just a week remains one of his deepest regrets to this day. Each time he recounts this tale, he begins with a mournful, "This has become the regret of my lifetime . . ."

Time waits for no one. If you miss someone, don't put off spending time with them; make that phone call right now. If you're young, it can wait until tomorrow, sure, but once you reach middle age, it's best to act promptly. If your loved one lives nearby, it's a blessing. And if a phone call leads to an in-person meeting, what could be better?

Now that I'm older, circumstances often get in the way of reconnecting with those I miss. Each workday in my office, the first thing I do is turn on my computer. I check emails, and then I scroll through my Facebook feed. One day, I received a birthday notification. I was completely taken off guard because it was for a friend who had passed away years ago. I left a comment on my friend's feed: "Happy birthday. How's life over there?"

This friend and I went to med school together. In college, one of his lungs was in such poor condition that he needed urgent surgery. Even when all of our friends went to a classmate's wedding, I was the only one to skip it because I wanted to be by his side when he woke up.

Reading through my friend's Facebook history, I found a comment from last year by the classmate whose wedding I'd skipped, wishing him a happy birthday. But this year, no comment from him, as he had also passed away.

More than half of my college friends are gone now. The remaining ones either live in nursing homes in poor health or suffer from mobility issues that keep them homebound. Sometimes I send out group emails to my college friends, and now only two people respond. Each time I check my inbox, I fear there may be more bad news waiting for me.

Loneliness is the enemy of a joyful life. The easiest way to combat this foe is to spend time with old friends. Time seems to fly when you're reminiscing about the good old days with friends, doesn't it? In old age, it's wise to keep those old friends close. They are living testimonies of your past achievements— your youthful vitality and lifelong accomplishments—that can help alleviate any feelings of emptiness that may arise with age. I can attest to the consolation you feel in the company of old friends who have weathered the journey of aging alongside you. So, if you miss someone, don't hesitate to reach out. Life is too short for hesitation and Rain Checks.

In our bustling, work-dominated youth, socializing itself might feel like a chore. Of course everyone would like to have the perfect kindred souls nearby, but your job might force you to meet people you don't want to, or interact with difficult superiors. Worse yet, if you're constantly accosted by those only seeking favors, you might be tempted to abandon everything and move to a remote mountain, completely off the grid—cut off from any social interaction.

One of the first things I loved about retirement was the freedom to choose. I no longer had to force myself to do things

I didn't enjoy. I could invest my time in people I liked and work I cared about, without anyone getting in the way. What a breath of fresh air! If I wanted to see someone, I would call them up without hesitation. I asked people to help with my projects without the constraints of professional titles or worrying about conflicts of interest. The support and friendship of the wonderful people I had in my life were the reason I was able to dedicate myself to research and volunteering even after retirement. Without them, and the enjoyment we derived from various projects, my later years could have been lonely and empty.

This is, unfortunately, one of the benefits you only get to enjoy in good health. Once in my eighties, I could no longer meet people as much, as I was so easily drained. There were also fewer people to meet, after all. So many of my friends have passed away, and those who are still alive usually have trouble moving about on their own. It's common for us seniors to lose touch. And there's no sadder thing, not too long after, to find yourself at the funeral of the person you lost touch with.

One winter day in 2014, I received an especially grim obituary. I was in Nepal at the time. I have a special bond with Nepal that was born first out of my fascination with the Himalayas, which I first visited in 1982 as part of a Makalu scholarly expedition. This bond grew only stronger once I established a volunteer group at Ewha University Hospital where I was teaching at the time, and we started volunteering in Nepal every year. In 2014, I had two significant events in the country. Three of my students, who had been part of the volunteer group since its inception in 1994, joined our twentieth annual Nepal trip with their families. My artist friends in Nepal—writers, painters, and musicians—also organized a book launch event for me, because it was the year when my Korean translation of

The Wake of the White Tiger by Diamond Shumsher Rana, a lifelong fighter for democracy in Nepal, was published.

With these two wonderful things happening at the same time, I was brimming with pride and anticipation. My wife and I attended the book launch with my son and his daughter. My granddaughter was engrossed in her smartphone, thanks to the impressive Wi-Fi connectivity in the Himalayas. In the middle of the event, I borrowed her phone to check my emails for any urgent matters. My heart sank when I saw an email with the subject line "Forwarded: Obituary." I knew I couldn't make it to the funeral even if I opened and read the email right then. I decided to put it out of my mind until I was back in Korea, but accidentally clicked it open. The message took my breath away: it was the news of my best friend's passing.

There's an old saying, "Spring has arrived, yet it feels not like spring" (봄이 왔건만 봄 같지 않다). That's exactly how I felt reading the news. What was unfolding around me in Nepal should have filled me with joy, but my heart was heavy instead. Because I was in the midst of the book launch, I couldn't share my feelings with my family and had to keep them to myself until the day ended. Even now, I vividly remember the devastating shock I felt.

My friend's name was Park Doe Il. We met when we were thirteen, and had been friends for over sixty-five years. When we first met, Doe Il was precocious beyond his years and a walking encyclopedia. In our buzz-cut middle school years, we started a book club under Doe Il's leadership and once a week, we'd sit around the table, discuss books, and listen to vintage vinyls together. Doe Il had a soft spot for Camus, a great influence in South Korea back then, and would read his books out loud. Doe Il would even analyze convoluted symphonies to us with admirable fluency. I believe my love for poetry and visual art has a lot to do with Doe Il, my dear friend from those formative years.

There was a time when Doe Il attempted suicide by over-dosing. Upon hearing the news, our book club gathered and a strange debate ensued. One member, who would later become one of Korea's most respected writers, argued that we should respect Doe Il's decision because ending his life was his choice alone. I think this absurd debate about life and death was sparked by our adolescent minds—sensitive, intellectually curious, and volatile. I interjected, pointing out that we had no way of knowing Doe Il's true intention unless we could ask him directly. For that to happen, Doe Il needed to survive, a counter-argument that gained the majority's approval.

Always a deep thinker, Doe Il studied philosophy in college and carved his own path in life, despite his perpetual questioning and self-doubt. Up until two years before his passing, we would meet almost every week to enjoy a meal of udon and reminisce about our old days. Udon was our go-to snack in middle school with our thin wallets, and it always brought back memories. But in the year before Doe Il's death, our schedules never aligned and we didn't meet at all. If I had known our friendship would end so abruptly without proper closure, I would have done everything in my power to make time for a little get-together. The regret weighs heavily on me, but there's nothing I can do about it now.

What does it mean to be alive? When you stop breathing and your heart ceases to beat, you are biologically dead. But isn't there truth in the cliché that as long as you remember and miss someone, they live on in some way? My friend Doe Il may have passed away, but I remember him as vividly as if I had seen him yesterday. I remember him as the passionate young man with a delicate heart who lived for art. I cannot express how much my life has been enriched and filled with precious memories because of this one friend. How fortunate I was, to have met him and been his friend in this life! Now all I can do is look up at the sky and say, "You made my life happy, my friend."

I believe that our true legacies are not inscribed in headstones. Some people, fearing oblivion, have their past titles, lines from a poem, or famous quotes engraved on their tombstones. But whatever you choose to inscribe will not endure forever. Even what's set in stone won't be remembered for good. The only inscriptions we actually leave behind are the good memories we create with our loved ones. If I can make someone else's life a little happier, wouldn't my life have been worthwhile?

Many of us make it through each day by holding on to the happy memories we've made with our loved ones. My reader, how do you want to be remembered? Don't you want to be remembered as the person who was an essential part of someone else's happiness? With these questions echoing in our mind, how could we ever forget every day is a chance to leave that inscription behind?

2

The Rat Race? Been There, Done That

In 1981, at the height of South Korea's nationwide industrialization, LG built a television factory in Huntsville, Alabama. KBS (Korean Broadcasting System), one of the biggest Korean broadcasters, documented and broadcast the process, from construction to operation. The film embodied the national sentiment of patriotic support for burgeoning Korean companies.

It's been more than forty years now since I watched the documentary, but one aspect has stayed with me. The Korean executive in charge of the factory visited the house of one of his American employees for an interview with his family. The executive told the employee's wife: "I'm grateful for all the hard work your husband's been putting in for our company. I'd love to repay in whatever way I can, so please name your reward."

I wondered if she'd ask for a big raise or a fat bonus. But instead, she answered: "Sir, I ask you to send my husband home on time."

At the time, I was speechless. Back then, Korean society was so focused on the single goal of working tirelessly to make our country and people prosper. A breadwinner who made ever more money was the ideal head of the family. But this woman would pass up this big opportunity just for the timely return of her husband?

A friend of mine, pushing ninety, now likes to say in a remorseful tone: "I really didn't need to work all that hard."

He tells me how his workaholic lifestyle drove his wife and children away. Many Koreans of my generation, I'm afraid, would echo this friend of mine. Our country's growth-driven culture asked many of us to make great sacrifices. And we always urged ourselves to work harder, not to fall behind, and to beat our competition. We propelled ourselves forward as if we were being chased. When the slow, bucolic stability of our agricultural society vanished overnight, an era of competition seized everyone without a moment of respite. Unsurprisingly, at one point, the number one cause of death for those in their forties in South Korea was overworking.

Regrettably, not much has changed. Though I'm heart-ened to see, in recent years, the term "work–life balance" has gained traction in Korea, hinting at our modern aspiration to strike a balance between professional and personal lives. This balance is now one of the most sought-after factors for young professionals in the job market. I view this as an ultimately positive trend that's gently steering our society toward a better direction. But it leaves a bitter taste in my mouth when I reflect on how this very trend serves as a stark reminder of our persis-tently competitive and overworked society.

My wife often tells me that the whole of her thirties and forties felt like a decades-long brain freeze. She cannot remem-ber much from that time, having spent every single day swamped with so many things to do as a working parent with four kids. And I couldn't agree more.

I had a chat with my eldest son a while ago. He told me that when he was in elementary school, with both me and my wife away at work, he never felt at home in his own home. A latchkey kid, he felt responsible for three younger siblings. As a father, I couldn't put into words the kind of guilt I felt for having put my son through so much stress at such a young age.

The era of overworking and the rat race must come to a close. Yes, now is a time not for survival but for a good quality of life! Have we not put behind us the era when long hours of underpaid labor led our economy? We should look toward the future, when only creative minds will be able to foster a thriving economy. And fostering creativity requires enough time for rest and leisure, boldness to take a chance, and room for trial and error.

On the other hand, I dare ask: Have we all been working to death, not of our own volition, just for survival, to make a living? Why did we sacrifice our youth and obsess over work?

When I first started working at a psychiatric facility, the reality of South Korea's medicine couldn't be further from the ideals I learned in school textbooks. As a teaching doctor at Yonsei University Severance Hospital, I couldn't even find acceptably translated medical texts to teach my students with, and was reminded of how I had struggled with foreign texts when I was at medical school myself and desperately hoped for translations. But no one had even attempted the grim task, so I took matters into my own hands. With my limited English, I had to constantly consult a dictionary and toiled over my translation; when, after much blood, sweat, and tears, it was published at long last, it became a handy tool—a rarity—for many nurses and counselors, not to mention mental health practitioners.

In the 1970s, inhumane treatments in psychiatric facilities, including restraints and closed wards, were still the norm in South Korea. Overseas, the open-ward system was gaining momentum, but no one dared to attempt such drastic change in South Korea, in fear of strict hospital regulations and skeptical guardians. Thankfully, I managed to talk the university into giving me full authority to run the hospital as I saw fit; confident that a better environment helps mental health patients improve, I became the first to operate an open-ward system in psychiatric facilities in South Korea.

All this was challenging work, but I looked forward to going to work and loved my job. I felt like a farmer plowing a field full of stones when I worked to apply medical theories in real life. So I feared nothing, and jumped on a new challenge every chance I got. That all-obliterating sense of focus and fulfillment left me thinking of nothing else at times. Had I been only after money or fame, I wouldn't have thrown myself into work quite the same way.

There are so many people who say they wasted their youth working. Of course, you might feel regret about missing out on other things while you were focused on your career. But you should first ask yourself why you were so career-focused to begin with. Didn't you find a sense of purpose, pleasure, and fulfillment in work, at least in the beginning? Were you not proud of who you became as a professional? If so, you shouldn't deplore but praise yourself. One of the greatest pleasures humans can enjoy comes from work. To have that to your heart's content—shouldn't you count yourself lucky?

If you still feel regret, it's perhaps because you didn't actually choose to devote yourself to your career but simply felt obligated to adopt that lifestyle. Many of my patients over the years were forty-something men who suffered symptoms of burnout. They all wanted to find themselves through other means than their careers. But most of them failed, not because of lack of time or resources, but because they themselves were not even sure what those other means might be. No matter how desperately they wanted a better work–life balance, their cries always ended up bouncing back in vain. You see, for a balanced life, you must first know who you are.

"Am I happiest working?" "Am I happiest interacting with people and building relationships?" "What allows me to be me?"

Those who can answer questions like these don't wind up in a meaningless rat race. Because they don't feel the need to defeat others and come out number one at the end of the race. They just focus on what they want to do, and on their own terms. But those who don't have answers to these questions tailor themselves to others' standards. They try to keep up with the Joneses. And when they look up someday and regretfully ask themselves why they worked so hard, their youth is long gone.

Not everyone knows what it means to work hard. By which I mean, the pleasure you get from working hard is a reward reserved exclusively for those who know who they are and have found meaningful work. If what I've said so far describes you, my reader, then cut yourself some slack and appreciate your hardworking nature. The good news is that work is a lifelong mission. And just because you're retired doesn't mean you need to stop working. If you've so far missed out on the meaning and pleasure of work, why not start now? Find the work that's truly meaningful to you, and see what joy it brings you.

3

The Unique Challenge of Parenting

B ACK IN THE 1980S when the democratic movement was at its peak, the South Korean college students leading protests and the police repressing the protests with brutal force were constantly clashing. A senior professor of mine happened to be passing Seoul Station during one of the protests, and stumbled upon his daughter who was protesting at the picket line. His heart skipped a beat. It's not that he didn't understand why his daughter was protesting, but he was worried she might get hurt. After a moment's hesitation, my senior professor bought a pair of sneakers from a nearby marketplace and handed them to his daughter, hoping to prevent her from getting injured by running around in her heeled shoes. Because of this little act of parental love, he was interrogated by a secret intelligence service agency. He was accused of having encouraged the protesters. It's laughable, but such was our world back then.

Anyone could understand how worried parents often get over their children's safety. But when you contemplate their safety in the long run, it becomes difficult to unequivocally determine what's best for them. Should you respect their autonomy and the choices they make? If so, what could you do to help, as a parent? These are the conflicts that many parents—if not all—face when trying to raise their children the best they can. And in such a situation, my senior professor decided that, though he was worried about her safety, it was in his daughter's best interests that he bring her a pair of comfortable shoes to put on rather than expect her to abandon a protest and a cause she believed in.

Parenting is quite the task, because there's no manual. Every parent has a different personality, every child a different temperament, and life surely leaves each family to deal with different circumstances. In short, it's case-by-case, which makes it impossible even for the most competent expert to offer fool-proof ways to deal with complicated parenting problems. So it's in the hands of the parents, and you will have to think on your feet and rise above the occasion, again and again. Sometimes you might realize that you don't even understand your children that well.

Let me tell you a story from my parenting years about my eldest son, who is now an astronomer. He got interested in stars long before elementary school, and my family always had this big debate about how he came to become obsessed with stars at such a young age. Around the Korean holiday season, I used to bring my young son to visit my former mentor, and he'd sit down and ask my son a lot of questions. Based on these little Q&A sessions, he reached this conclusion that my son, with both of his parents away at work until late, had nothing to do but stare up at the stars at night. In short, stars were probably manifestations of my son's separation anxiety and some sort of imaginary friend. Spoken like a true psychologist.

But I didn't agree, to be honest. When I was little, I'd climb up a persimmon tree to pass the time. After Korea's independence, my mother was often out volunteering. Back then, I was a sensitive crybaby who took everything personally. Whenever I missed my mother, I'd climb the persimmon tree and onto our house's roof, just to sit there alone, crying.

The Unique Challenge of Parenting

Still sentimental about those times, when my family got a plot of land in Deungchon-dong to build our house, I installed a ladder leading right to the rooftop so my children could play there. At night, it was the perfect spot to observe all the constellations. So, naturally, I guessed that my son began dreaming of becoming an astronomer because of my foresight and the makeshift rooftop observatory I had built. I secretly took pride in having played a role in my son's dream.

But you know what? We were all wrong! It turned out his dream started when we lived in Dapsimni, on the outskirts of Seoul. My son would play with his friends in a small alleyway, but they would be called home, one by one, around sunset. He'd always be the last one lingering there, looking up at the sky until my wife and I returned from work. He discovered that one bright star would always be the first to appear at nightfall. He wondered about the name of the star, but none of the teachers, nor my wife and I, could enlighten him. Then one day, he was looking through a student magazine and found out that the "star" was actually the planet Venus. That's how he first became interested in stars, and when Apollo 11 landed on the moon, he made up his mind to become an astronomer.

Of course, many different factors must have contributed to this dream of his. But the reason he chose, out of all those factors, was his curiosity. It wasn't separation anxiety as my former mentor believed, and it wasn't because I'd provided him with a house where he could watch the stars. He simply discovered the presence of stars at a formative point in his life, became curious, and studied them. That was all.

If you're a parent yourself, my reader, you'll surely know how surprisingly often your children remember past events differently from how you do. My children frequently don't remember what I considered a big gesture on my part, and some events that have entirely escaped me have become lasting memories for my children. That's the tricky part of parenting.

What you strive to provide doesn't always reach your children, and what you didn't give a second thought to sometimes ends up affecting them more than you could have imagined.

To tell you the truth, the time my family lived in Deungchon-dong has never been a happy memory for me. Back then, it was a district hastily developed for those in desperate need of housing, specifically because of overpopulation issues, and naturally, not a great neighborhood for families with little kids. My children had to cross a road without a proper crosswalk to take a bus or climb a hill to go to school. Unpaved roads would turn into muddy pools whenever it rained. I was working at Yonsei University Severance Hospital at the time, and it always bothered me that my dirty shoes left muck all over the clean floor of the hospital after commuting through the rain. Whenever I got to work, I headed straight to the bathroom to clean my shoes before anything. What's worse, because our construction company went bankrupt, our house was abandoned halfway to completion, with the front gate missing. I felt guilty about raising my children in such an unsafe environment and always worried about them.

To my surprise, however, I found out that my children remember that time with great fondness. They told me how they saw pheasants and snakes on a hill on their way to school, and even befriended chipmunks and birds. On empty lots where foundations hadn't been poured yet, they played in a pack with the neighbor kids until late into the evening. Without the front gate, my family got along with the entire neighborhood as if everyone were related by blood. What I always remembered as an unsafe neighborhood, in fact, had been a playground to my children, surrounded by all that nature had to offer.

What does it mean to raise children well? Parents want to do everything in their power for their children. But there's really no guarantee that your efforts will do your children good. They will take what they need, not what you want them to take, and build their own worlds. Let me put on my doctor hat for a moment. If our parenting prescriptions so rarely impact our children's upbringing in the ways we intend, then, is it even fair to think we do the hard job of parenting for them? Apparently, our children do their own hard work, growing up around our decisions. Speaking from experience, when parents live their lives to the fullest, their children grow strong in the soil of those good lives and take as much nutrients as they need. Which is to say, you don't need to try to model whatever idea of "good parenting" you hold at all times, because, in the end, if you live your own life to the best of your abilities, you naturally become a pretty decent parent for your children—and that's all they need.

When I first started working at Ewha University Hospital, it was just an outpatient clinic, without its own ward. Under my guidance, we opened a small ward with a capacity to hospitalize up to twenty patients, and I brought my children there often. My relatives were appalled that I'd take my children to a mental health hospital, and lectured me. But what's wrong with educating my children about where and how I work? I never thought of treating mental health patients as a stigma that I should keep my children from, and it didn't feel right to automatically consider those with psychological and neurological conditions potential threats. So my children continued to accompany me often on my workdays, and were quite pampered by the staff and patients alike.

On Christmas or a holiday, my children performed in a play or choir for the hospital staff and patients. No one told them to. They just put their little heads together and came up with these ideas, which brought a smile to my face for sure. Sometimes these surprise performances were imaginative, sometimes so surprisingly insightful that we adults would be forced to take long looks at ourselves. And my children joined us—hospital staff, patients, and their guardians—as special guests for outdoor excursions in the spring and autumn. The time we spent together provided the patients with valuable opportunities to reconnect with the world outside the hospital, an unexpected benefit. And my children gained a lot from navigating the unique circumstances of these events.

At Ewha University Hospital in 1974, I introduced psychodrama as a way of treatment, collaborating with the playwright Oh Young Jin, Professor Rhee Kang Baek, and director Kim Sang Yeol. My eldest son in particular was influenced greatly by these early interactions with creative thinkers and artists. Oh, whom he called "Grandpa," told him many mythological stories about stars. Rhee even showed my son his early drafts of a play that was yet to be made into a stage production, and would offer critiques on and show genuine interest in my son's youthful attempts at a novel. Even now, my eldest son has a great love for books and plays, and enjoys spending time at art museums, no doubt a reflection of those formative experiences in his early years.

You know, I didn't have a hidden agenda to teach my children such valuable lessons when I brought them to work with me. What I did, in fact, was just share my everyday life with them, in full. And I didn't exactly intend for this firsthand workplace experience to be a defining moment in their lives, but simply wanted to spend as much of the little time I had as I could with my children. But they soaked up this experience, in this new environment, and made it their own. I didn't raise my children well, my reader, but they did a great job growing up. That, I'd say, is the mystery of parenting.

So, reader, you shouldn't keep looking back and regretting the parenting choices that you might wish you could change.

You see, parenting is tricky in so many ways. In old age, with your parenting years behind you, you might realize just as I did that not much really went as planned as you strove to raise your children well. Your assumptions about your parenting role—just as I assumed I'd influenced my son's dream—might even turn out completely off base.

I, for one, always found myself floundering with my children, even though I was fairly knowledgeable about parent–child relationships as a psychiatrist. Because of my overprotective mother, I always yearned for easygoing, cool parents. That's why I resolved to be the kind of father who would offer a wide, lenient boundary for my children and allow them ample room for trial and error, and life experiences. But guess what? Alas, my approach to parenting, as it turned out, felt borderline neglectful to my children!

In elementary school, my eldest son received an award from his principal. He had to walk home from school with his three younger siblings with only one umbrella to share during a heavy downpour. The story goes that my son let the rain drench him, while holding the single umbrella over his siblings all the way; the principal spotted them and commended my son for his chivalry. When I heard the news, I couldn't have been more proud. But you know what my son told me? He had no choice, he said begrudgingly, because with working parents, he was the only one who could look after his siblings. Just an elementary school student, he himself must have wanted to be pampered and needed someone to rely on, but emotionally, he felt like a boy patriarch—what a heavy load to carry! Yet instead of taking the time to truly understand his feelings, I was quick to praise him for receiving the award. What an immature father I was!

But who among us can really be faultless as a parent? All parents are amateurs and will end up making a few mistakes. There's no escaping it. But the good news is, our parenting decisions don't define our children. They have their own agency. Yes, I know you might find this hard to accept, but your children do their fair share of growing up and becoming who they are by themselves, just as much as you help shape the people they become.

Here's the comforting truth: raising children well is far simpler than you might think. The only thing required of you is to form and cultivate a great bond with them. And that's not so different from other human connections. You just need to be honest and genuine, and act like a decent human being, instead of pursuing whatever ideal image of a good parent you might have. When you do, your children will learn to accept you for who you are, for all your good qualities along with all your human weaknesses. They will build and grow their lives to full fruition, around that truthful parent–child relationship you offer.

As long as you parent by these principles, I see no need for distinguishing good parents from bad ones at all. In a sense, under these conditions, there's no such thing as a good or bad parent. There are only real parents who try their very best.

4

GET TO KNOW YOUR PARENTS

ONE SUNDAY, WHEN MY children were in elementary school, my entire family was at home unwinding and I decided to discreetly hide a small recorder in my pocket to capture our everyday conversations. When I played the recording back later, I was in for a shock. My kids were much quieter than I had always thought, and guess who was most vocal? It was me. And I sounded extremely bossy for that matter, strikingly different from my psychiatrist self. During our family meeting, I smoothly dismissed my children's contributions with a vague "Well, let's put a pin in that." Of course, it was just a ploy, because I had already made up my mind and was only asking everyone else's opinion as a formality. But since I was usually met with little protest, I had always considered myself a very democratic father, quite inaccurately, as the recording showed me.

That's probably why my children now have a habit of paying little attention to what I have to say. I do understand where they're coming from, but I also can't help feeling a bit torn about the whole thing. In old age, parents start holding themselves back more. They worry that their already busy, overwhelmed children might feel like they are being pushed around or that their involvement might be seen as meddling, or sticking their nose in, instead of taking some load off their children. So aging parents choose their words very carefully around their children. No wonder we end up feeling so sorry and torn when those words seem to bounce back without making any difference.

But what can one do about that? As a child, I didn't really listen to my father, either, and we rarely had a real conversation. My father passed away at forty-nine, in the middle of the Korean War. The war drove our once-successful noodle business to the ground overnight, after which our family of four moved from one dilapidated studio to another. My father drew his last breath in one of those broken-down studios.

I remember my ailing father losing weight and getting weaker by the day, but we never found out what was wrong with him since all the doctors had been drafted to the front lines. A high school student at the time, I managed to procure a prescription that we hoped could help and administered shots to my father at home for two years until he passed away. I burst into tears quite a few times giving my father shots and looking over his emaciated body, each day frailer than the day before. He used to be a man of impressive health, but near the end of his life, my father writhed with agonizing pain at the slightest touch of a needle. The heartache I felt for him in the grip of illness undoubtedly influenced my decision to pursue a career in medicine.

My father was a man of strong principles and rules, which he stood by as if his life depended on them. Back when he'd owned the noodle factory, his business thrived so much that he could afford to run a few more factories manufacturing essentials. He wanted to expand his business beyond Daegu, where we lived, and across the country. But he needed permission from the Japanese governor-general of Korea in order to make his plan a reality. He went through the complicated filing process and applied for the license, but was rejected over and over again. Back in the day, the right connections—a good word sent in—were often more important than legal procedures or formalities. But my father refused to cross that line and put his faith instead in the rules he had been told to follow. My uncle, having watched all this, stepped in one day and told him, "Brother, let me handle this." And he showed up with the official permit the very next day. I don't know what strings my uncle had to pull, but I bet my father was dumbfounded.

On the other hand, my mother was quite the warrior. She insisted on finishing high school and bent her opposing father to her will, and made a controversial claim that kimchi and soybean paste, homemade Korean foods, should be manufactured in factories. This challenged the long-held belief that these Korean staples, being soul foods, *must* be made at home. But my mother could not overlook the monumental amount of work and sweat that went into producing these foods at home, as kimchi and soybean paste were made annually in ample quantities to last a family for the entire year. For a family of four, for instance, thirty cabbages were needed for a batch of kimchi—a task sizable enough for a factory, in her eyes.

In short, my mother was a woman way ahead of her time. She just had to have things her way. So imagine how frustrated she must have been living with a man like my father! Owing perhaps to the tension from their incompatibilities, my mother had suffered from chronic stomach disorders throughout her married life and would often be bedridden. Always short on painkillers back then, some Koreans were forced to opt for morphine instead, and my mother was no exception. But once my father passed, she became healthy as a horse, with no hint of morphine withdrawal symptoms either. Years later, when I became a doctor, I could see her chronic illness was probably due to all the stress coming from the constant compromises she had to make for the sake of my father.

Under the guidance of such a strong mother, I grew up as a model student and always assumed I'd inherited my inflexibility—aversion to rule breaking of any kind—from my father. An only son with just one younger sister, I had to deal with my mother's overprotection on top of my own personality flaws, and would sometimes blame it all on my father when I felt cooped up. I would even dismiss him as a man who always prioritized his responsibility over his desire, an ordinary citizen who doggedly went with the flow and followed the crowd.

Years after his passing, however, I learned something new about my father. I'd always known that he had gone to the same high school as I did—Kyungpook High School—but I discovered that he was missing in our yearbooks. When I looked into this mystery, it turned out he had graduated elsewhere, at Mokpo Commercial High School. I couldn't understand. With such poor transport back then, why would he graduate in Mokpo, in another province? It turned out that my father was one of the students who led the March First Movement for Korean independence, and the school expelled all those involved afterward—forcing him to find a new school. I was dumbfounded. My father—a stickler for the rules—had been expelled?

Who knew my father was such a hot-blooded rebel? And how come he'd concealed this side of himself for the better half of his life? This discovery brought up an old, long-forgotten memory I had of my father. Usually so agreeable and gentle, there was one occasion when my father showed his rebellious side. When I was a mischievous little thing, only six at the time, I had fooled around during the solemn Japanese morning session at school, for which I got a beating and called *boollyeo-ngsunin*, a rebellious Korean (불령선인 / 不逞鮮人)—a derogatory, discriminatory word used to refer to Koreans who didn't comply with the Japanese government during the era of colonial rule.

When my father learned what had happened at school, he threw my bag out in the front yard, gathered all the textbooks from my desk, and set them on fire. He yelled at me to never think of setting foot in school again. During my time-out, I felt my legs trembling from all the shock at this man who had acted nothing like my father. My aunts didn't know what to do, either, and tried to calm him down in vain. Afterward, no one uttered another word about what happened, and I couldn't ever bring myself to ask him about his outburst. So the memory had stayed hidden, until my discovery of his expulsion.

Now I see—that outburst was a result of his pent-up frustration. His fury at Japanese colonial rule, fear he had developed during his activities for Korean independence, and despair and shame that had overtaken him since he gave up on the life of resistance and chose the easy path of an ordinary citizen. All of those feelings must have come to a head when his only son was mistreated and deemed a "rebellious Korean."

My deepest regret to this day remains that I never got to hear all these stories from my father himself. I could have gotten to know him and learned what his dreams were, how life failed him, and what he'd learned along the way. In my foolish youth, I was too hasty to dismiss him as a docile citizen who refused to venture outside the box and so I never thought to investigate who my father really was. How sorry—sorely sorry—I am.

Even while living in the shadow our parents cast, we hardly ever find out how they became who they are. What we think we know is just the tip of the iceberg, and most of us part from our parents without ever getting to see what's beneath the water. How can we understand our lives well without understanding our parents? Their life stories have hidden clues integral to understanding our own. When we come to see our parents as people with untold stories to share, we can finally understand the parts of ourselves that we inherited from them.

I promise, reader, that in your parents' life stories is a path of breadcrumbs to your own. But you can only find that path when you keep an eye out for these clues and hints and really try to understand their perspectives. Be inquisitive about your parents. Put aside your biases for a moment, and listen a little more. This is a sincere word of advice from one foolish son, who realized he'd never gotten to know his own father until long after his passing.

5

REMEMBER: REGRETS ONLY BEGET MORE REGRETS

A STUDENT OF MINE who had retired a few years before visited me one day. Some people suffer symptoms of "retirement sickness" more harshly than others, and he seemed like one of the more severe cases. He had everything it takes for a safe landing in great late years, but still felt anxious all the time. His body wasn't like it had been before, his memory had gotten worse, and he felt irrelevant in many of his important relationships, with no one to lend an ear. I told him that everyone grows old, not unlike him, and it's just the way of life, which only made his anxieties worse.

What could I have possibly said to put his mind at ease? I mean, in old age, you've got a lot to lose. Yes, your body's far from its prime. Some scholars even consider the aging process itself a pathological phenomenon. In short, they classify aging as a disease. Even simple tasks take a lot more exertion now that your body's grown old, and your mind has dulled. So, are there any good things about aging? Let me ask you—even with all these odds stacked up against you, if you manage to have in place a decent postretirement life plan, wouldn't you call that a blessing?

I tried to talk some sense into my student by pointing out how he had many more things in his favor than most. He'd made wonderful scholarly achievements, mentored many great junior colleagues to follow in his footsteps, and had enough savings and pension to live comfortably in old age, so he was better off than a lot of people. He even had a wonderful gig already and had been giving lectures and speeches at many venues since retirement. Even so, he still didn't know where all his best years had gone, and felt a lump in his throat whenever he thought about the future.

Although I was encouraging him to be more positive, I do understand those bitter regrets about could-have-beens and should-have-beens. And in old age, you may live in fear of approaching death. But that doesn't help anyone, of course. So, my reader, I'm sharing some of my own tactics to deal with anxiety in old age that have proved most effective.

First, accept your old age and set your mind to "despite" mode. Don't flatter yourself with people's meaningless comments such as "you don't look your age." Even if you really do not look your age, that doesn't mean you're aging any differently. Looking young and being young are two completely different things. How foolish it'd be for you to insist on being young, in spite of everything pointing otherwise.

Not a lot of things are at your advantage in old age. I can't exactly disagree if you say you have more reasons to be sad and depressed. But in "despite" mode, not everything will turn out to be so bad. Yes, *despite* your body and mind not being quite like they were before, you can still make yourself useful and contribute to society. I promise you—there's a mission for the rest of your life that you just haven't considered yet.

Everyone's present is a sum of past actions and choices. Everyone has knowledge and experience accumulated over the years. Yes, a great wealth you have yet to recognize, my reader.

Think again, and examine whether or not you're undervaluing your own life experience and accomplishments. Big or small, those fruits of your labor are of value. If you don't value them enough yourself, how can you expect others to respect you for what you've done with your life? Remember—accept your changed reality in old age, but also take advantage of your great wealth. Yes, whoever you are, in your old age, you have a wealth of valuable experience and knowledge to offer to the world, *despite* all your disadvantages.

Second, don't rush into things; do things "bite by bite." Once you recognize your wealth, it's time to put it to use. By not rushing, I do not mean you should stall. Don't overcomplicate things and just take action, but remember to do so "bite by bite," even if you don't feel like time's on your side. Things need to fall into place as a natural course of events. So, relax and enjoy the process—it's gonna be fun! In old age, it's essential to embrace the joy of process instead of getting fixated on results. If you lived a life of competition in youth, don't you think you deserve some reward? Here's the secret: the reward is that very joy you can find in the process of doing things "bite by bite."

The perks of "bite by bite" are rooted in a lighthearted approach to life. "Bite by bite," just as an April shower soaks through your jacket. Take your time, and you'll have the pleasure of discovering in every experience some new things that didn't catch your attention before. The more often you find something new in the ordinary, the more joy there will be in your life, with even more joy to follow.

Third, don't compare your own life's yields with those of others. Jean-François Millet's painting *The Angelus* captures a moment of prayer as a farmer couple stand side by side over a basket of potatoes in solemn gratitude at the end of the day. I feel this painting portrays the essence of an ideal life in old age. That serene acceptance of the year's yields and a moment of deep gratitude. The humility to take things as they are and bow their heads in the face of all of their hard work that has finally come to fruition.

In old age, every one of us needs to accept life for what it is and learn to be grateful. The peace and contentment we're promised in old age come from nothing but that very acceptance. My reader, don't go wasting your remaining years getting hung up on the past and anxious about the future. Stop thinking "I wish I'd manured my field more in the spring," "Is this all my yield," or "Other people's crops seemed better than this," and instead think of ways to make good use of what you have right now.

I'll say it again: the best thing about aging is the freedom you have, without all the responsibility and obligations of the past. What was your life like before retirement? Didn't you work like a racehorse, in order to make a living, for a bigger check? You barely had a moment to look around or look back on yourself in this world that's always cheering us on with a scoreboard overhead. One of the things that can let you down in old age is your regret about the roads not taken. But your postretirement life is a great time for you to go on that second journey and enjoy a newly found sense of freedom, following your heart. You shine when you're not trying to be someone else. Even if you have only one more day left to live, it's your life: yours to make or break. You can put into practice all the lessons and theories you want in old age, but here's a tip for you: it's better if you start early in the second half of your life. Our future is as important as our past. But neither counts without our today. You're the architect of your own happiness, and you can draw up your blueprint today.

A close friend of mine once vented to me that he'd never lived his life on his own terms. Whenever he was at a crossroads, when he should have followed his heart, he was too afraid to change and always resorted to going with the flow out of fear. But of course, he's far from alone in this regret. It is, in fact, one of the most common regrets that I hear from people. A doctor friend of mine who works at a hospice conducted a thorough survey of his patients and not following their hearts turned out to be the number one regret by a landslide—to no one's surprise, really.

To be fair, my reader, regrets tend to be stickier than contentment, so they stay with you much longer. No matter how you've lived, you'll always look back on the road you did not choose and feel inevitable regret and curiosity. But does regret actually mean you've chosen wrong? What do you think—does a feeling of regret cancel out all those years my friend has lived the best he could, and render the entirety of his life an empty shell?

Everyone's born with an inherent temperament to some degree. Even newborns have different dispositions. Right after birth, a nurse will insert a medical instrument in a newborn's mouth to remove particles and secure the airway, and some newborns, sensitive by nature, burst into a loud wail, while others just frown a little.

And of course, we all want to live in accordance with these temperaments we're born with. Sensitive people would not want an overstimulating environment, while the energetic ones might seek out dynamic environments where they can express themselves loud and clear. But we can't choose our environments. We cannot choose our parents, race, or country of birth. Environments are givens in anyone's life, something we need to adjust to. In that process of adjustment each of us forms identities and a clearer sense of self. Sometimes you're required to comply with your environment and sometimes you're allowed to be true to yourself and change your environment, all of which contributes to this complicated end product of a self. In short, life is a sum of all such decisions you've made, balancing between your nature and environments.

Whether regretful or up to your expectations, it is your life. Whatever your past looks like, it's surely a journey no one else in this world has taken. Your life is a unique piece of art, created by no one but yourself. Inimitable, truly one of a kind. Treat it with the respect that it surely deserves, and do not talk it down out of all that regret pestering your heart. My reader, there comes a time for us to confront, accept, and admire our own lives. Buddha, we're told, said the day he was born in the gardens of Lumbini: "In the whole universe, only I exist" (천상천하 유아독존 / 天上天下唯我獨尊). Didn't he shout for all of the world to hear that every one of us is unique, irreplaceable, and literally singular in this world? If you have to learn one aphorism by heart, learn this one and remind yourself day and night.

The aforementioned friend regrets that he's suppressed his true nature out of fear of what people might think. But think about this. Do you think it's easy to follow the herd and lead an ordinary life? My generation went headlong through the ups and downs of modern Korean history, from Japanese colonial rule and Korean independence to the Korean War and subsequent split of the country in half. In the world of brutal poverty and war, survival was our top priority. We worried what to put on our tables for the next meal, and had little choice when it came to making a living. Individual sacrifices were taken for granted, because, my reader, it was that kind of time—time of little means and great sacrifice. But if you've made it through all of it, made it out alive and well, with your family doing OK—isn't that alone quite a feat to achieve? You've built this life from the ground up, so don't you deserve some recognition and applause?

Do you still feel regretful, my reader? Are you still thinking about that road not taken? What you feel you missed out on, of course, will always be more obvious in your heart than what you didn't. Here's my solution: take that road now. If you've always tailored yourself to your environment, now it's time to live in harmony with your nature. Didn't I tell you? One of the best things about aging is freedom. If your dependents are grown up, and you're more or less financially stable, now it's time to finally follow your heart. Instead of reminiscing and regretting, the more productive way to deal with all this is to get started on whatever you wanted to try with your life, right this second, bite by bite, day by day.

Two decorated former politicians were deploring their current life situations on a park bench. One of them said, "I didn't heed anyone's words of advice, and look where I ended up!" And the other replied, "Damn it, I was always swayed by people too much and look where that got me!"

Regret comes with life, however you've lived. Even if you've led a successful life and you find yourself content, you might still envy someone else's more unique life. But don't let the poison of regret set into your life. Accept the decisions you've made so far, because your life is the result of your having lived the best you could.

Believe me, every single one of us has thought at some point: "What have I lived for?" or "Was I really the captain of my own life?" But no matter what, however you've lived, you have been the captain of your own life. Because being a captain of your own life is not about you being happy with the result of all those little steps you've taken in life's journey, but about the very fact of your having taken those steps, for your own reasons, till now—which is irrefutable. Face this truth that your life was indeed *your* choice, so you can move on toward your tomorrow. No one can live two lives at once. And the life you chose—it wasn't that bad at all, was it? Take some pride in that.

PART 3

SECRETS TO HAPPILY EVER AFTER

1

Atonement

O VER FIFTY YEARS OF practicing psychiatry, I've worked with tens of thousands of patients. Some of them came to me with light symptoms, and some with far graver ones that got in the way of their everyday life. But unlike physical conditions, psychological ones cannot be easily diagnosed based on outward symptoms. There are too many variables throughout the patient's life that could have developed into the symptoms acting up at the moment. Even after a formal diagnosis, I always agonized over which path of treatment would be best for each patient. Newfangled equipment might be the indisputable answer to diagnosing physical conditions and how they can be improved, but it takes a long time for a doctor to decide whether the treatment's really working for psychological conditions. And that process has been one of solitude and much challenge, with no exception.

All doctors, when it comes down to it, work with life and death. So of course, the pressure a doctor feels on the job is beyond words. For other professions, you might have a chance at redemption even after making wrong decisions, but a doctor's mistake might cost a life, which is irrevocable. It happens, naturally, that we tend to carry some of our patients in our hearts long after meeting them, along with deep regrets that we could have made a different choice, handled the situation better, and saved them.

I carry a few patients in my heart. While I was an army doctor, someone I'd examined for enlistment a few years before came into my office one day. At first glance, I could tell he was a serious patient. But the diagnosis I had given him as a trainee included a speculation that I suspected a made-up health problem. It still happens, but back in the day, we had numerous cases of "draft dodgers" who feigned serious medical conditions in order to avoid being enlisted. I felt a penetrating sense of remorse. I shouldn't have jumped to conclusions, and should have gone through additional tests to ensure the accuracy of my diagnosis. It broke my heart to think how many years that young man had been forced to spend in the army, facing disadvantages and suspicion, just because of my insubstantial diagnosis.

I once had a committed patient of clinical depression who requested an overnight trip out. Since she'd been a hardworking patient with years of good work under her belt, and her symptoms were much lighter now, I greenlit her night out from the ward. Of course, I made sure to explain the various risks to her grandparents who came to pick her up, and the rules for them to keep in mind at home. Right after they drove away, I got a phone call from her mother, who was away in the countryside at the time. She'd had an ominous dream the night before, and pleaded for me not to approve of her daughter's leave. I reassured her, "Don't you worry. As a doctor, I'll make the decision in the patient's best interests." But that night, my patient jumped from her apartment window to her death.

Ever since her death, I've harbored this inexpressible guilt and regret in my heart. I kept thinking to myself I should have listened to the patient's mother. And what I'd said to that patient's mother that night remained lodged in my heart like a sharp dagger, a festering wound.

Remorse, in a sense, is a self-imposed sentence. Even when there was no legal liability or even formal complaints from my deceased patient or her guardian, I sentenced myself to a well-deserved punishment according to my own private moral trial. I've punished myself with years and years of agonizing remorse.

Life without regrets sure sounds great, but unfortunately, such an impeccable life is not a real possibility. Of course, we can all avoid causing intentional harm, but we are far from omniscient deities; we can't but make some mistakes, even doing our very best. Even those actions I regret the most, in truth, were never meant to cause harm. I wonder how much unintentional pain I must have caused my whole life, and how many mistakes I would have made unknowingly. The list would be endless, if I were to count all the wrongs I didn't even think much of, or am not even aware of.

My good friend and Nepalese doctor Rajbhandari once took me hiking on Kalinchowk, a mountain in Nepal. We climbed hundreds of stairs to the mountaintop, where there was a Hindu temple. We meditated for a little there, and decided to make our way back down on the other side. On our way back, we had to climb down hundreds of stairs, just as we did climbing up to the temple. Before I could take my first step, Rajbhandari asked, "Doctor Rhee, have you ever sinned?"

I hesitated for a moment. Since I couldn't think of a time I actually meant anyone harm, I answered, "I don't think so . . ."

He explained. "It says sinners will be cursed climbing down these stairs."

Our entire way back, my legs kept shaking and my body was stiff all over. Rajbhandari eventually burst into laughter and confessed he was just joking. But joke or not, I broke out in a nervous sweat during our hike down for all the world to see.

Yes, I must have sinned, even if unknowingly. Consider this for a second. Life itself is a process of exchange. Even those who claim to owe nothing to anyone owe their very existence to this world. For starters, where does our drinking water, food, or the air we depend on come from? We owe these crucial sustenances to other forms of life on this planet. How much life has been sacrificed and ruined for the sake of our survival? It is our human destiny to hurt something, someone, simply by existing. So who am I to say that I have not sinned?

The Nepalese set the average life expectancy at a hundred years, which they divide into four phases of twenty-five years each. The first stage ranges from birth to twenty-five years old, during which you're raised and learning. The second stage is from twenty-six to fifty years old, during which you put into practice what you've learned in the first stage. The third stage is from fifty-one to seventy-five years old, during which you have to atone. The fourth stage is from seventy-six to a hundred years old, during which you'll liberate yourself from all worldly affairs. We'll come to the fourth phase later but, for now, let's focus on atonement. Why did the Nepalese argue for remorse in this third stage of life, when you'd ideally be spending the little time you might have enjoying the fruits of your labors, and some peace of mind?

Here's why. The influential twentieth-century psychoanalyst Erik Erikson identified eight stages of psychosocial development that every person would pass through over the span of their life. The last of his eight steps takes place in late adulthood, from sixty-five onward, and highlights the importance of ego integrity. To have ego integrity means you are able to accept your life as it is and as it was, in all its good and bad. Which is to say, he argues for a healthy, positive attitude with which to evaluate our life when we look back at this age, despite the mistakes and wrongs we've committed throughout. Yes, just like the Nepalese. Only when we achieve ego integrity can we face the approaching end of our lives with calm and not succumb to utter despair. We find a true sense of freedom.

Hence in old age, my reader, every one of us must repent. You shouldn't just simply count your past wrongs. You should really look back and survey your life for all the unintentional harm you could have caused, all the people you could have unknowingly hurt, and even the sins you glossed over without thinking much of it. Even all the shame and remorse you have kept deep down—that's also part of your life. And accepting the whole of it is the crucial first step to spending your last days in bliss.

2

THE HAPPINESS OF FORGIVING

ONE DAY, A MIDDLE-AGED woman came in for a counseling session. She told me that her mother-in-law was dying, but she still couldn't find it in her to forgive that dying woman who had put her through such a hard time when she was a newlywed. She even went so far as to say that she still shuddered with rage at the mere sight of her in-law's emaciated face lying limp on her deathbed, which brought all the terrible memories rushing back like it was yesterday. She would try to calm herself down, repeating, "Let's treat her well, she's not long for this world," and yet at the sight of her mother-in-law, she'd still feel a hot knot of rage coiling in the pit of her stomach, her throat closing. Her emotional distress, it seemed, was getting to her body and it was showing.

As a psychiatrist, I've met a lot of people with broken hearts: those with emotionally abusive or financially usurping parents, cheating spouses, business partners who stole from them and ran away, in-laws who turned out to be exploitative bullies . . . Whoever the inflicters, the victims all suffered terribly. They all complained about the feeling of resentment and anger hardening and weighing down their hearts. And believe me, you cannot do any good by bringing up forgiveness to these patients. Some might rush into telling these patients, "Why still suffer? It's been long enough for you to let go." But that's just rubbing salt in the wound. Yes, they might be talking about wrongs that happened in the past, but their suffering is in the present tense.

Forgiveness, to say the least, is not easy at all. Often, the one you resent tends to be someone close. It's rare to be hurt so badly by someone you can easily disengage from. To be hurt by someone you have to see on a day-to-day basis, sometimes someone who loves you, will cut the deepest. Often, we tend to find ourselves in a love–hate relationship with the unforgivable. It's difficult to go cold turkey on a relationship like this. You might end up hurting yourself trying to cut someone like this out of your life.

What's worse is when the ones who inflicted so much pain in the first place don't recognize the level of hurt caused. To them, what's past is all in the past. Even if they apologize, they rarely seem to take it seriously. Or, perhaps worse, they may never offer any kind of apology. They might even act nonchalantly and blame you for holding grudges. This kind of shamelessness further provokes the hurt ones. For them, life goes on as normal, while victims end up with the burden of forgiveness.

So forgiveness is no easy task. Religions and prophets have always emphasized the importance of forgiveness, because it is, in fact, extremely difficult to forgive. But you need to forgive at some point. If you don't, you'll be the one left in that hell of resentment, still hurting, with no end in sight. If my patient failed to forgive her cruel relative, it wouldn't be her mother-in-law but she herself who would continue to suffer. Which is to say, forgiveness is a choice you must make for your own sake. To paraphrase the Buddhist saying, resentment is like a hot coal you hold in your hand just to throw it at someone, but it is you who ends up getting burned.

The burning of resentment doesn't always grow into an impulse to take action or revenge on the person who hurt you. Sometimes, its fire consumes just you and your life, all of it. So even if it's not easy, you need to learn to let go of your resentment. You mustn't waste your short life and limited energy on hating someone. No matter what, life essentially is about your happiness. If you want to be free to pursue happiness, you need to approach this matter of forgiveness now. You need to learn to forgive.

But of course, it's not a feat you can achieve overnight. Even when you're starting to feel better, the very next moment you might find yourself simmering with rage, and even when it seems out of your mind entirely, you might suddenly find yourself trembling with anger again. So you cannot rush into forgiveness. Forgive little by little, as much as you can at a time. I recommend the following three steps for those who have decided to forgive someone.

First, disengage. The more resentful you are, the more you might want an apology. But it's rare for the perpetrator to kneel before you and beg for forgiveness. Stop that thought—that you'll forgive on the condition of an apology. Even forget that decision of forgiveness itself, and just distance yourself from the feeling of resentment altogether. Keep yourself from the memory that hurt you so by being decidedly indifferent. You first need to protect yourself from that toxic feeling of resentment by no longer waiting for the apology.

Some might ask what to do if they need to face the perpetrator every day. Of course, it'd be easier if you could cut them off completely. But what's more important is your psychological distance from the painful memory. As the saying I once heard goes, "To carry a grudge is like being stung to death by one bee." Resentment builds when you constantly remind yourself of the pain and make past injuries your present. My patient felt all the ways her mother-in-law had wronged her like they had happened yesterday. In that vicious cycle of resentment, it is only you that gets hurt, over and over again. Shift the focus of forgiveness from the perpetrator to yourself. Make the decision to put the crucial distance between yourself and your burning resentment, all for your own sake—not theirs. That is the first step you need to take in order to forgive.

Second, once you've disengaged and have more room for reflection, try to study your trauma from a new angle. When you're able to put some distance between yourself and that painful memory, you'll have more room for re-evaluation and understanding. This is of course not to say the inflictor's wrong magically disappears once you come to understand their perspective, but the feat of forgiving without forgetting becomes possible when you newly understand how you came to be injured.

Third, forgive yourself. Let me tell you a story from my youth. I used to pay a visit to my old professor every big Korean holiday, and with my limited finances at the time, I had trouble finding a decent gift to bring along. Since I couldn't afford fancy holiday gifts from a department store, I wanted to at least bring something thoughtful. That's how I hit upon the idea of orchard apples. I went to an orchard on the outskirts of the city, picked the best apples I could, and went to my professor's house with a bamboo basket full of them. My professor warmly welcomed me and graciously accepted the gift. Then, a week later, I had a chance to visit his house on another occasion, and saw my basket in the corner of his living room. Seeing me stare at the basket, my professor's wife explained with a smile on her face, "Oh, it turns out there are still country bumpkins with such old-fashioned tastes in gifts."

Her words pierced my heart like a poisoned arrow. Afterward, I never prepared any gifts when visiting my professor's house. I resented them for having humiliated me despite my best intentions. Back then, so humiliated and hurt, I thought there was no excuse for their behavior. I couldn't find it in myself to truly forgive my professor's wife. Whenever I saw her, I kept thinking back to that moment with the basket.

But with so many years and so much experience under my belt now, I wonder if it was really something for me to forgive in the first place. When I was younger, there was a clear line between my wrongs and others'—what I needed to apologize to others for and what I expected others to apologize to me for—but as I grew older, the line became more and more blurred. Who forgives whom? Let me forgive myself. If I don't forgive my resentful, angry self first, who would forgive me for all my wrongs?

Looking back, I see that my professor's wife was just being honest. But I took her honesty personally. By forgiving myself, I mean that I forgive myself for having been so small-minded and having distorted the honest words of my professor's wife into a personal attack, and for having resented her for so long based on that single incident. Only then did I find myself free of the trauma of my "old-fashioned apples." Had I been able to do so earlier, I would have felt so much freer. I regretted wasting the time I could have spent enjoying a better relationship with my professor and his wife.

Forgiving others is only going halfway. Forgiving myself—that's the undeniable, complete forgiveness. And complete forgiveness means liberation. Liberation from the resentments that imprisoned no one but yourself. In *War and Peace*, Tolstoy wrote, "If you think someone has wronged you, forget it and forgive! And then you will know the happiness of forgiving. We have no right to punish."

Why not make up your mind to forgive that person who wronged you? Maybe you're not ready right now, but give it time. Disengage, reflect, and take another look. Only when you're truly free of resentment can you be at peace with your life. In old age, you realize that forgiveness is an assignment you cannot put off forever.

3

GOOD COMPANY ISN'T
THAT HARD TO FIND

IN CHUNCHEON, SOUTH KOREA, there's a place called "The Inconvenient Cottage." And what an inconvenience indeed—you need to take the local bus that runs three times a day, the only means of public transport around the area, to get to this cottage nestled in a deep valley. Without working plumbing, warm showers are out of the question and you'll have to make do with a quick, cold wipe-down by the little stream outdoors. With the kitchen rudimentary and dish detergent entirely prohibited, you'd better get used to steamed potatoes, as they will make up most of your meals there. For nature's call, there's a neat outhouse, where you need to sprinkle ash and shavings after you're done for the natural composting process. There's no shop in the vicinity, and the cottage comes unequipped with a TV or radio.

The cottage was built by Choi Sung Gak, writer and environmentalist, with his organization, Nature Peace Lab. He opened this cottage in order to give us city people a chance to take a long look at our thoughtlessly wasteful modern lifestyle. In exchange for such inconvenience, guests find valuable gifts during their stay: birdsong, the melody of the stream babbling by, all those little winged insects and grass bugs, wildflowers like daisy fleabanes and daylilies, and the quietude and comforting ambience a city life just can't give you.

I first met Choi back in 1999 when he founded an environmentalist organization called The World of Flowering Plants. After he moved to Chuncheon, I soon heard about The Inconvenient Cottage and visited him there with my son. It was a cozy, heartwarming place, I could tell, with a novelist's romantic touch. After our overnight stay, I kept thinking about the cottage, and finally, one autumn day a few years later, I sent him a reservation request by email. I told him one eighty-something, one seventy-something, and one sixty-something would be visiting, and got this response: "Three old souls, noted."

And I replied: "No old souls, just three thoughtful boys at heart."

The other two boys at heart, apart from myself: Park Jong Rock, a fellow older alumnus from when I was studying cultural studies at The Cyber University of Korea. He was known for his diligence and wholehearted dedication to the growth of provincial communities. The other was Ban Eul Seok, who had brought to one of my book events a copy of my first book with rigorous notes and invited me to a passionate discussion on life quite a few times. Having worked overseas for a long time, Mr. Ban was now retired and leading a quiet life back in Korea with his wife.

We three became good friends after a trip to Nepal together in 2015. We all lived by the motto, "Even if we die tomorrow, life should be fun, on our own terms," and would always go out of our way to invite each other to whatever we were up to. Our desire to preserve curiosity and excitement about life bonded us so much that we started laughingly calling each other boys. To save ourselves some face, reader, we also dutifully added the adjective "thoughtful," which we stood by.

We planned a three-day road trip to The Inconvenient Cottage. Just like youngsters nowadays, we went Dutch for all our travel expenses, instead of sticking with the customary Korean way that expects the oldest and most financially stable to pay. Sure, we were not used to this, but for us old men, it can be fun to imitate the youngsters now and again. For our first stop, we swung by a spicy stir-fried chicken place that came highly recommended by Choi Sung Gak. And we just fell in love with the owner. Without our asking, the owner would dart around to serve us more side dishes even before we ran out of them. Anyone who walked into the diner could tell the owner really cared. On the wall it said they deliver everywhere in the country. One of my acquaintances, a licensed caregiver, happened to be volunteering at a nearby nursing home. I had five servings of the stir-fried chicken delivered to the home, hoping to surprise my acquaintance—and in return for the owner's hospitality.

We arrived at The Inconvenient Cottage late in the evening, and hung out with Mr. Choi deep into the night. How good it was to break out of our daily city routines and just relax! We counted the stars and chatted like little boys. As Mr. Choi himself said, "This cottage is a house built of poems." That night was a dose of poetry in and of itself.

The next morning, we set off for Goseong, but first made a stop at the National Mountain Museum in Sokcho. The museum curator gave us a tour around, and the museum proved to be a fascinating place. But I also found out that it lacked artifacts to showcase South Korea's long history of hiking, as opposed to foreign mountain museums that display old records and keepsakes from famous hikers. I asked the curator if I could donate a few things in my personal possession. For the record, they were not of much value. Just a photograph of me and Sir Edmund Hillary, the first man to ever reach the summit of Mount Everest, and his autograph, and the rock Nam Sun

Woo—a legendary Korean hiker—took as a souvenir when he single-handedly climbed to the top of Everest, and a dried edelweiss from Khumbu gifted by the Nepalese mountaineering guide, Ang Dorje Sherpa. The curator graciously accepted my donations, understanding how I hoped my small contribution would become the beginning of a growing collection of keepsakes at the museum.

On our way back home from our three-day journey, I got a text from my acquaintance thanking me for the stir-fried chicken. But I was the one that should have thanked him. How blessed I was to have all these people in my life, and how that very fact made my trip an unforgettable time. Mr. Choi built a place where I could cherish Mother Nature to my heart's content, and thanks to the other two boys at heart, I had the most memorable, joyous trip. And what about that owner of the stir-fried chicken place? Because of his excellent cooking and great service, I had another chance to send a surprise gift to my acquaintance and share another grateful moment. And let's not forget the curator—who didn't take my suggestion of donations the wrong way and added the items to the museum's collection, with much generosity. All I did was invite two people on my trip, and yet I was rewarded with joy much bigger than I imagined my small action would entail. I have so much to be grateful for, don't you think?

Why am I telling you this story, dear reader? To show that as you age, you should strive to be sociable rather than solitary, whether you're traveling, studying, or volunteering. As your daily life becomes more mundane, the radius of your activities shrinks and your social connections become sparser than in your youth. What makes old age truly challenging? I'd say it's social isolation. In order to cure this curse of loneliness, you have to seek out good company. And how do you do that? The easiest way is to spend time doing something together. Do you want to go on a trip? First, try picking at your brain for a marvelous getaway destination. If your destination is great, like-minded travel companions will naturally join your journey. And when you really pick at your brain, there must be a name or two in the entire nation you could invite to join your trip. Don't be shy and get in touch. Start small. If you've enjoyed a dish, share it with someone later. No matter how trivial it may seem, the act of sharing itself is what matters. Who'd reject someone so caring and inviting?

Some people envy me, assuming that I belong to many social groups and my friendship runs deep. Indeed, many seem to mistake me for some kind of social butterfly who manages to make genuine connections with people. They assume that I've got my life perfectly together and have some great magnet-like personality that just attracts people left and right without much effort on my part. But it's not like I always have people knocking at my door. The truth is, I'm usually the first one to reach out to people. My secret is to keep it simple and humble. When you overthink and try too hard, you hesitate to take action. Just share what you can in the moment, be it a plate of good food or some historical keepsakes, and invite people to be part of whatever captivates you there and then, just as I invited my friends to join my trip. That's less pressure for everyone, and that kind of interaction will prove to be much more in your favor. When there's no pressure, you have a better chance of nurturing that first encounter into a more meaningful connection down the road. This seemingly insignificant philosophy is how I've managed to continue to build and enjoy wonderful relationships even in my old age.

There's no perfect time to connect with someone, nor are there always the right things to share. Sharing this very moment, now, and doing what you're about to do together, is the best way to connect. And sharing is the best way to keep people close.

Before you complain about loneliness, rack your brain first, because, I promise, there will be a person or two you can fall back on in times of solitude if you look hard. Do not overthink. Just invite them out lightheartedly. Such a simple gesture can often lead to joy beyond words.

4

FIND YOUR SAFE HAVEN

I'VE BEEN GOOD FRIENDS with Rajbhandari for thirty-eight years. When we first met, Rajbhandari was the president of NEA (Nepal Epilepsy Association), and asked for my help in solving the problem of an antiepileptic drugs shortage. So I started to donate medications to Nepal, and he's the reason why I founded the official volunteer group based at Ewha University Hospital and started organizing yearly volunteering activities in Nepal.

Now that I'm old, I've passed the baton; my former junior colleagues have taken over and lead the annual trip to Nepal, but I've stayed in touch with Rajbhandari through it all. Last year, he wrote to me to share some great news. He's been a rigorous practitioner of meditation for all the years I've known him, and he had finally received the certificate for completing the highest level of meditation training.

When we first met, he recommended meditation to me. He told me quite a few times that if just 1 percent of our global population meditated regularly, we'd be living in a much more peaceful world. I followed his example and tried out various forms of meditation—from the cross-legged style to a jumping one—in order to find inner balance. The times I spent hiking, praying at temples, and meditating with him remain some of the most enriching moments in my life.

My life as a psychiatrist in South Korea has always been hectic. I often grew heavyhearted myself when listening to my patients articulate their pain. Our competitive modern society doesn't allow us to reminisce or look back for long. My generation in particular was busy enough trying not to fall behind. Of course, I've found myself feeling drained and empty from time to time. But reality never failed to corner me into the same hectic day regardless. What I discovered in Nepal was the luxury of a lighter heart. Surrounded by the Himalayas, I reveled in the generosity of the Nepalese, who taught me to sometimes take a step back and relax. I could truly unwind. That's probably why people kept telling me I looked different after my trips to Nepal. And I couldn't agree more. Without Nepal, my spiritual hometown, I would have burned out well before my retirement.

One day in Nepal, Rajbhandari and I passed a Bhairav statue in Kathmandu Durbar Square. People stuck coins to this statue and paid respect, holding their palms together. As soon as they finished praying, little kids swarmed over the statue to collect the coins. But the worshippers left as if nothing had happened, despite clearly seeing all this. I was perplexed by their unfazed reaction despite this disrespectful behavior, and asked Rajbhandari if I was missing something. He answered: "The worshippers dedicated those coins to the god. The coins now belong to Bhairav, not them."

He meant the coins that left their hands were no longer their business, and what happened to the money was now up to the god. At his wise words, a scene from the past flashed before my eyes.

In Korea, on Buddha's birthday, I once paid a visit to Gwanchoksa Temple in Nonsan. Worshippers formed a long line in front of the Maitreya Buddha statue for offerings of light. A middle-aged lady, I saw, contributed a particularly big candle and would not step aside for the next person. With that kind of crowd, it's customary for a worshipper to politely stand aside right after they make their offering, but she would not budge. As I continued to watch, a female Buddhist monk came over to use this lady's big candle to light her own, and the lady snapped at the monk to not touch her candle. She seemed to believe that the monk, by taking a lick of the flame, had stolen her good luck.

In our modern society, we often find even the culture of tribute and worship has become one of competition, which surely leaves a bitter taste in our mouth. But Nepal was distinctive to me in its perspective on worship and tribute. The Nepalese never ceased to question what truly belonged to them, and remained vigilant of the agony and unnecessary conflicts that a greed-oriented mindset can entail. Thanks to this Nepalese viewpoint, during my stays in the country, I learned to curb my pestering greed that had gone uncensored before. Owing to my meditation training, I could also control my self-centered impulses much better once back in Korea.

Six years ago, in Nepal, I visited Dolka for the first time in twenty years. This mountainous village is the place our volunteer group chose for our first trip, and back then, it was secluded and unpopulated. At the end of my day, I would climb Kalinchowk. Halfway up the mountain there was a hut where a yogi was meditating, and at the top, an unmanned Hindu temple. While climbing the mountain in this sublime, untouched quiet, I always felt like I was in a god's arms, and every step was a meditation of sorts.

But Dolka had flourished beyond my wildest imagination in the twenty years since my last visit. There was now a paved road leading straight to the Kalinchowk base that a small vehicle could drive on. The trip that had taken days before was now only hours long. So I changed my plan to stay in the village and drove to the mountain. Where there was once the yogi's hut, I saw a number of houses that served as guesthouses and cafés. Kalinchowk had become a thriving tourist attraction. It was a truly different world.

The environment hadn't changed much, though: the plants and flowers along the road, sounds of faraway and nearby wildlife, blue sky, wind, and quietude. I found the spot where I used to meditate twenty years ago and rigged up a little tent. Society might have changed, but not the essence of the Himalayas. I let myself take some good rest there, facing the anxiety, fear, anger, and emptiness that had been brewing within me as I aged. My agitated mind slowly came to a peaceful lull. A smile crept across my face. I couldn't stay long with my altitude sickness kicking in, but I felt more in my element there than anywhere else in the world.

Everyday life in the modern age is hectic. And what makes it so hectic is usually out of our control. You cater to your company's needs in order to make a living, and build your life around your responsibility and duties to your family and dependents. So it's not all that surprising if you ever end up feeling alone and empty from this ringing question—where's my life, and who am I in all this?

The late British psychiatrist Anthony Storr said that life is a coin with two sides of opposing desires.[3] One drives us to form connections with people. The other inspires us to return to our true selves in solitude. This binary exists not just in social relationships but also in our professional and romantic relationships. We grow through our responsibility and duties and learn to find joy in sacrifices and helping others, but deep down, we all also wrestle with an irresistible desire to live for ourselves. Life becomes a bleak landscape when we fail to keep balance between these two conflicting desires. We all need that sense of balance—to carry out our duties while not losing ourselves in the process.

Which is to say, I thankfully have two worlds. I feel, so to speak, I can let my hair down in Nepal, where I get to take my mind off worldly affairs, after which I return to South Korea and live my regular life without burning out. Living with tunnel vision is bound to lead to exhaustion. So I always remind my students and fellow doctors of the importance of having a place and time of one's own. I remind them to not forget themselves because of their overwhelming responsibilities and duties. You may not need to go as far as Nepal, but let me tell you, my reader, it's better to find that crucial safe haven sooner rather than later. When you find yourself in a dire need of respite, if or when the tides of loneliness and emptiness begin to lap at your feet, it's likely to pose a great challenge to come up with one out of nowhere.

It's been forty-two years since my first trip to Nepal. And how much has my time there changed my life for the better? With my remaining days so short now, I don't know how I could ever repay the kindness of the Nepalese. All I can do is to offer another prayer for Nepal and the Himalayas. My safe haven.

5

My One True Best Friend

"I'VE BECOME QUITE DISFIGURED because of you. My neck grew so long waiting for your letters, and my right arm grew longer from all of my love-letter writing."

This is a quote from one of the love letters I wrote many years ago to my wife. One day she brought it out for me to read in front of our family. My children giggled uncontrollably at these cheesy, cringeworthy lines, because they could not believe the writer was me. My wife and I haven't been exactly lovey-dovey around our children, so they never would have imagined I had this romantic streak.

But that was exactly how I'd felt at the time of writing that letter. I met my wife when I was fourteen. She was a friend of my younger sister, so she was always over at our house to hang out. Throughout our school years, we treated each other like siblings.

But everything changed once she left for college in Seoul. One day, I heard that someone had set her up on a blind date. The moment I heard that news, I couldn't stop my heart anxiously beating against my chest. I was transfixed with the realization that I could not let her get away. I ran to the post office and bought a hundred greeting cards. And then I started sending a letter courting her every single day.

The one my wife brought out was one of those letters. I haven't dared to revisit my letters from those courting years, but I know I must have poured my heart out and said goodness knows what kinds of things. Eventually, moved by all my efforts, my wife ended up marrying me.

Though we started off with all these romantic words, our life together didn't get off to a great start. First of all, I was dirt poor. Since my father passed away and our family business went bankrupt, I'd been living in debt. What's worse, I served time in prison for having been a student leader of the April Revolution, a democratic movement against then-dictator President Rhee, and after I was released, I had a hard time finding a job. With my limited finances, we started our married life in a studio flat, and spent our honeymoon in a tent up on a mountain. Even now, my wife sometimes playfully asks me how the hell I had the guts to ask her to marry me. I don't even understand it myself. But if I knew how much hardship I would put her through in years to come—before I finally secured a stable job—raising four kids and looking after a mother-in-law, on top of her own studies, I don't know if I would have been bold enough to propose at all.

Over time, little by little, we worked ourselves out of the red, but still my wife couldn't expect an easy life. In retrospect, I've always been a bit naive when it comes to monetary matters. My mother never discussed money with me, probably protective of her only son. Perhaps that's why I'm still no better than a child with my everyday finances; I have no idea how much a decent house costs, what our monthly expenses are, or which bank offers the best interest rate and so on and so forth. My wife has always been the financially savvy one, who's had to make big and small financial decisions instead of her husband, who knew nothing about money. Growing up, my children often complained about how my wife never loosened her purse strings, but her frugal nature was necessitated by marrying me, who had been poor and too lenient with matters of money.

Even so, I always bit off more than I could chew, throwing all my caution to the wind. I donated medical supplies and even a building while doing volunteer work for Nepal and the Gwangmyeong Orphanage. As a psychiatrist, I introduced new treatments such as psychodrama and art therapy, which all required funds to back up. As if in a pact, those committed to a meaningful cause were always in need of an increased budget. And I always strived to contribute as much of my own resources as possible—be it time, knowledge, space, or money—when those in need came looking for help. As a result, my wife has always ended up the victim of my financial whims. If I'm a tunnel-visioned idealist, my wife is the voice of reason who carefully navigates between her ideals and reality. If it wasn't for her, I would have filed for bankruptcy a long time ago. Some people laud me for being a humanitarian, but those who really know me always compliment my wife on her saintly patience.

And let me tell you, my reader, I do sometimes wonder. How come my wife stayed with me—a man of so many shortcomings—for nearly sixty years? I suspect it's because we had a similar vision as scholars. We share our important values, as a sociologist and a psychologist, respectively. We both believe in the significance of a healthy relationship between individuals and society at large. Society and individual—it's a chicken or egg kind of deal really. Happy individuals make up a healthy society, and a healthy society keeps individuals happy. Knowing this all too well herself, my wife never stood in my way. She has always been supportive of even my costly projects. Truth be told, my wife even went so far as to plan and participate in most of my projects herself. If it wasn't for her, I wouldn't have been able to carry out numerous missions I started, from volunteering and studies to education. Our common goal of making the world a better place—rather than focusing on ourselves and our own interests—bonded us, more strongly than we ever could have imagined.

I admire my wife. Above all else, I respect her as a scholar named Lee Dong Won. A sociologist, my wife has a bird's-eye view over any situation, always helping me zoom out instead of delving into the mind of an individual, which is my first instinct as a psychiatrist. She's always led our family as a strong, self-aware woman, so I've had the fortune of practicing a family model of relative gender equality. She is the very reason why our house gate proudly bears both of our names. She's the reason why I taught a Women's Studies course at Ewha University Hospital, a first time for the school. And the reason why I received a Family Values Award back in 1999 for my work, unusual for a Korean man of my time.

And I admire the Lee Dong Won who is a mother of four and my wife. Under such challenging financial circumstances in our youth, she had to juggle her studies and the task of raising children. My wife tells me that those rough patches taught her how to set her priorities, find inner balance, know when to give up, and, sometimes, when to persevere till the better days came. When I look back on our history, I feel a surge of respect and sympathy from the bottom of my heart for my wife, who managed to draw such glittering wisdom from the depths of one tough life.

Whenever I'm asked to officiate a wedding, I stress the following three pieces of guidance. First, have all the fun you can. Second, be creative. Third, help each other grow. Fortunately, my wife and I have satisfied all three our whole marriage. We made up our own creative ways to deal with our poverty and had fun raising kids, studying and working together, and helped each other grow in our respective fields of study—our married life couldn't have been better.

My wife is now as old as I am. Her eyesight's worsening, as is her hearing, and she's grown reticent along the way. Sometimes I even doubt we're understanding much of what the other has to say, but it's all good. When accompanied by my wife to an event—a lecture or a lunch—I often have a surprising experience. She will blurt the very thought that's on my mind. That's when I feel deep in my bones, yet again, all the years we have spent together. Of one mind, of one heart. About whom else could I ever say that?

Remember, reader, the three pieces of guidance I give newlyweds. A union of love is all about sharing joy and learning from each other. It was through our shared vision and mutual growth that my wife and I got through the roughest patches of our married life.

What a relief to have my wife by my side, my life companion and scholarly comrade. She made me who I am, and I made her who she is. More than sixty years after we first met, thinking back on our life together, I feel as if I'm transported back in time and am once again that young man writing fervent love letters. I feel an urge to sort through those old postcards my wife's kept all these years. Till my last day, it's always her to whom I want to give the world.

6

BRIDGE THE GENERATION GAP

WHEN THEY WERE LITTLE, my grandchildren sometimes refused to go to nursery. Having to get to work themselves, their parents—my children—fussed over them and always found some way to coax them into the car. On a day like that, I saw my grandchildren making faces that seemed to be saying they're complying just this time, but begrudgingly, and only out of love. But my busy, tired children didn't always seem to catch those looks, those silent signals my grandchildren were sending. They probably didn't have the experience or luxury of time to sit down and talk through what was going on inside the little heads of their own children.

It was no different for me and my wife. We were always amateur parents, even with four kids, since each required different parenting skills. What's worse, my wife and I were both working parents and had little time to spend with them. Time flew past us, year after flitting year, and I still can't figure out where all those years went. When our kids were all grown up and we had a little more time on our hands, we finally had a chance to look back and realized what rookie mistakes we'd made over the years. But regret couldn't have changed anything by that point, our hair already salt-and-pepper.

But fortunately, as a grandparent, I had the experience to be able to tell when my grandchildren were having a tough time. Whenever my wife and I felt their refusal to go to nursery was more than a mere tantrum, we stepped in. And my grandchildren always had good reasons when we asked why. On such a day, we would take our grandchildren out on a little field trip of our own, hand in hand, listening to them. After an excursion like that, they no longer seemed so on edge.

A while ago, my eldest grandson got married. Yes, the very first boy who graced me with the beloved title of Grandpa! It feels like it was just yesterday that I stood holding him in my arms for the first time, my chest swelling with all the love I felt for him, but that little baby grew up so fast and was now starting his own family! When he first came over to introduce his wife, I was so happy that I felt as if I could fly through the sky. You see, when my own children settled down and got married, I was worried sick for them and couldn't relax enough to be happy, but with my grandchildren, it was pure awe and joy.

Really, the joy my grandchildren brought into my life is beyond words. More than anything, it's because I finally learned the joy of parenting when I was helping to raise my grandchildren. I still feel sorry for my wife and children over all those years back when my children were growing up and I didn't do the best job of providing for them or being present, as I was working away from home as an army doctor or serving time for my involvement in the April Revolution. Meanwhile, my wife had to carry the heavy load herself. Even when I got a stable job at a hospital and started bringing in a decent income, it didn't come close to being enough to support our family of seven—me and my wife, our four children, and my own mother. I went to work at the break of day and came back at dawn, without time to think about anything else. Time passed in the blink of an eye, and then, suddenly, all of my children were grown up.

But then I met my grandchildren—these amazing mysteries of life squirming in my arms! They learned to sit, stand up, walk, and then even run—and all this came to me as a total surprise, as if I'd never seen anything like it before. When they started to speak and mumbled out a barely audible "Ganpa," I teared up despite myself. Whether they were mischievous or troublemakers, they always remained the apples of my eye.

When I was a little kid myself, my maternal grandmother doted on me so much she took to patting my head and giving me a big hug before affectionately bursting out, "My sweet baby!" This was probably imprinted on my memory, because I'd also blurt out, "My sweet baby!" whenever I saw my grandchildren. My reader, I even brainwashed them! When they were little, my grandchildren came to visit me every weekend, and I made them greet me with "I'm my grandpa's sweet baby" instead of the ordinary hello. As soon as they set foot in my house, I'd holler, "You are," and my grandchildren would holler back, "Grandpa's sweet baby!" And the whole family would break into laughter.

Oh, but the short-lived joy! Once my grandchildren were in elementary school, they would refuse to holler back, acting shy. They'd just smile and give me a short hug. My youngest granddaughter once even asked: "Grandpa, am I not my dad's baby? Why am I your baby?" And so our unique greeting came to an end. Now that all of my grandchildren are adults, I sometimes whisper into their ear, just in case, "You are," and they whisper back, "Grandpa's sweet baby." I mean, what a golden bond to share!

But here's the thing. No matter how much I love them, my grandchildren live in a completely different world from the one I or even my children grew up in. I grew up listening to my grandparents' stories in their laps, but my grandchildren had childhoods nurtured by the internet and its connected world, listening to various content accessible online. Between us there's bound to be a generational gap, of course. If you let that gap grow, it will soon become a gulf. And how could you—or anyone, for that matter—love someone you don't even understand? At the heart of every love lies this desire and determination to understand. And I wanted to provide that crucial opportunity for me and my grandchildren to understand each other. My reader, how I tried to fit in!

So I started emailing my grandchildren my childhood stories: back when I thought I was Japanese due to imperial Japan's extreme policy to obliterate the Korean nation, the despair of having no future during the Korean War, and my adolescent years when I'd climb up in a persimmon tree and contemplate who I was. My grandchildren were bewildered and delighted by these stories, which felt, to them, like historical events from the textbooks coming to life. And through our correspondences, I learned a lot from my grandchildren, too. They would comment on my emails, using slang such as 냉무 *naengmu* (lack of content), 헬조선 *helljoseon* (hellish Korea), 워라밸 *wolabel* (work–life balance), and 소확행 *sohwakhaeng* (small but sure happiness). My grandchildren enlightened me with these Korean acronyms and taught me all about the brewing social issues behind them.

In this age of nuclear families, people rarely live with their grandparents anymore. So children's ideas of family are pretty limited today. With declining birth rates, most of them have a sibling or two at most—which is to say, to them, families mean groups of five people or fewer, most likely.

Smaller family units can lead to children who might tend to be more individualistic and self-centered, their world so much smaller. Their parents, accordingly, may give their all to raising their single child or couple of children. In Asian countries, a term has emerged to describe a side effect of this societal phenomenon: "Little Emperor Syndrome." It literally means that children act like emperors ruling over their parents and grand-parents, and have them under their thumbs.

I once got into a taxi, and the driver complained to me about his grandson. He chided his grandson for misbehaving one day, and the kid fled to hide himself in his grandmother's arms and asked her, "Grandma, there are seven billion people in this world! Why did you choose such a bad guy to marry?" I couldn't believe my ears! I mean, the kid was precocious to even bring up the global population, but the snide way he blamed it all on his grandfather, rather than thinking back to what he could have done wrong? What a kid! And what if no one ever succeeded in disciplining this boy? Would he still be murmuring "Why this bad guy of the seven billion people in the world" when he got negative feedback from his supervisor at work? What about all the future hard times and difficult circumstances that wouldn't be to his liking? He would surely find it hard to fit in anywhere.

Many scholars and experts predict that in the future many of the traditional jobs we have today will disappear. But they also agree that there's a uniquely human ability that's unlikely to be replaced by AI. It's empathy, or EQ, broadly speaking. In our individualist society of a growing number of one-person family units, people with superior EQ will be more and more highly sought-after. But how do you improve your empathetic skills? By connecting and forming deep bonds with others.

The crucial role of grandparents in our modern age is to teach their grandchildren these empathetic skills. When I was a little kid myself, Korea was still bustling with little town-level communities, so all our neighbors were really one big family. This community spirit helped instill in us respect for others' feelings, and codes of behavior. Kids these days, living in more sparsely knit, individualistic communities, don't get this ben-efit. So what grandparents can do is help to expand their social world. Sure, you can just give them pocket money now and again, but why stop at that passive role? Engage with them, tell them stories from your own childhood so they have some understanding of what the past looked like, and be the connector between them and the wider family—with their cousins and young relatives.

But you have to get creative as well. However good your intentions, if you fail to engage your grandchildren, all of your well-intentioned words will end up being received as unwanted sermons. First, befriend them. In order to be friends with your own grandchildren, or any young people for that matter—whether your grandchild, child, or family friend—my reader, you need to try really hard to understand their world. You need to figure out what they respond to. Trying to understand another person's perspective—that's the beginning of all great love.

7

ACCEPT YOUR PARENTS FOR WHO THEY ARE

LIFE RARELY OFFERS UP its wisdom on a silver platter. That's why we always hear the regretful "If only I knew then what I know now." The youth, armed with passion and bravery, lack in experiential wisdom, and the elderly, with all their experience and insight, no longer have as much opportunity to put it to use. This irony of life rings true not only for parenting but also for children's relationships with their parents. If I'd have known then what I know now, I would have tried harder to understand my mother better; I would have been a wiser man— if I could just go back in time. It still makes my heart ache to think how much hurt I must have caused my mother at times. How well do we really know and understand our parents?

My mother, as far as I remember, was the strongest person I've known. She had a heroic spirit and never backed down when it came to something she believed in. During the Korean War in the 1950s, injured soldiers piled into my elementary school, which quickly reached full capacity. We students left the school building so that the soldiers could be treated there, and studied in a temporary classroom rigged up near a cave where people made roof tiles. It was a time of great challenge, and most people had a hard time just taking care of their own family. But my mother volunteered to take care of the injured soldiers at my school and war orphans at orphanages. Afterward, she went on to live her whole life as a selfless volunteer.

While my mother was widely loved and respected for her philanthropy, I always found her difficult and even terrifying. She had a clear sense of right and wrong and was relentless in pursuing what she wanted once she made up her mind, so I knew I had no chance of swaying her over anything. I grew up under her unwavering guidelines for safety. Anything that could bring even the smallest harm was prohibited. I wasn't even allowed to go swimming or play football. When I misbehaved, my mother called me aside, sat me down, and reprimanded me in a low voice. She never got emotional, but instead scrutinized my wrongdoing with infallible logic. Whenever I was told off like that, I wished she'd just hit me instead. It caused me so much pain to hear my mother scold me that way.

I felt I would never escape my mother's shadow. Sometimes I wanted to run away. Once I got accepted to a college, I straight out told her: "Mother, your love is too great and grave for me to bear, so please tell me the price of your love. I'll pay off my debts my whole life."

Back then, I desperately wanted her to give me the exact value of her love's gravity in Korean won. In my childish mind, no matter how much, the calculable sum must be less burdensome than the weight of her intangible love. My mother sat in silence for a while, and finally said, "You'll see when you've got children of your own. That's my answer."

Many years later, when I was married and a parent myself, I finally realized what I'd done to my mother that day. What nonsense—to ask your parents to calculate the price of their love. How saddened my mother must have been to hear her son making such a demand. The frustration and guilt I felt toward my mother over this incident have remained a significant *hua tou* (화두)—subject of meditation—throughout my life.

An avid Buddhist, my mother got in the habit of visiting the temple from time to time when I was a young resident doctor. By the time I had children of my own, she'd started to go out in a dyed Buddhist robe and stay in a temple for a few days at a time. I started getting phone calls from friends and relatives, asking after my mother.

"Did your mother become a monk? I saw her at a temple . . ."

I was embarrassed whenever this happened, because I felt as if they were accusing me of not taking good care of my mother and pushing her away into the arms of a Buddhist temple. My reaction must have stemmed from me feeling like a bad son and guilty about that past incident, of course. I wished she would stay home and take care of my children more often, instead of going to the temple. Sometimes my mother would hear my wish and stay around for an extended period of time. But whenever she did, she would be bedridden not long after. It had been the same way when she was younger. Whenever my father bent her to his will, she suffered terrible stomachaches. No matter how old she got, she was who she was. She needed to live her life on her own terms—that was in her nature.

Defeated, I accepted my mother for who she was. I told her she should live as she saw fit, and set her free. Just as she had shown understanding and patience for my adolescent protest all those years ago. Once I did, my mother was soon out and about, as healthy as before. There she was, my one, true mother again—going out in her dyed robe, with nothing but a backpack flung over her shoulders. I find myself proud of my mother beyond words.

She passed away at the age of eighty-four. My whole life, the best thing I've ever done for her as a son was saying those simple words that set her free.

It took me so long to finally accept my mother for who she was. Had I been able to do that sooner, had I seen her not just as my mother but as a *person*, even a little bit earlier, we wouldn't have ended up hurting each other so much. Though full of regret, I know I cannot go back in time. After all, I needed to go through all that—from my childhood in the shadow of my strong mother to my own fatherhood that finally gave me a chance to understand parental love—to finally, truly understand my mother.

When you're older, there will come a time for you to have to accept your parents for who they are. Remember, whether parent or child, we all start off as novices in this relationship. And all novices are bound to make some mistakes. Which is to say, we'll end up hurting each other one way or another. If not irrevocable, if not truly unforgivable, we should be ready to understand and forgive each other for the hurt we've caused. You should put the words and actions of your parents in context, by lowering your expectations and seeing them for who they are: human. Only then can we finally escape the long shadow cast by our parents. Only then do we find ourselves truly independent adults.

Parents and their children, from the moment they meet, are the closest any human beings can possibly be. They will influence each other for years to come, and yet, ironically, might never get to know each other that well. But we do, if we're lucky, have the time to get to know one another. It may take you a lifetime to really understand your parents. Try to look back on your parents' lives before it's too late. This is the last chance for you to let yourself heal and finally make up with your parents, who might have hurt you without knowing.

PART 4

THE UPSIDE OF AGING

1

IF TIME IS GOLD,
THIS IS YOUR GOLDEN AGE

HERE COMES THE ERA of centenarians! The Boomers, who were born between 1968 and 1974, are expected to live to one hundred years on average. Back in 1970, the average life expectancy for Koreans was sixty-two years. It's truly beyond our wildest dreams how the world has changed.

The first time I had come across the notion of a lifespan of a hundred years was in 1982, when I was introduced to the Nepalese division of life into four stages of twenty-five years each. Back then, the concept of centenarians was not exactly in everyone's dictionary, so the Nepalese perspective was refreshing to say the least. At the same time, I was reminded of Erikson's eight stages of psychosocial development, as I mentioned in an earlier chapter. You see, science and spiritual teachings often have surprisingly similar insights to share with us.

But still, most of us took "centenarian" to be new terminology referring to an improved life expectancy and nothing more. But now the era of centenarians has become our reality. In 2009, in its report on aging, the United Nations virtually officialized the era of homo-hundreds, which is to say, of centenarians. A few years later, in 2015, the UN also announced guidelines for age distinctions in the era of homo-hundreds. According to the announcement, childhood lasts from one year to seventeen years old, adulthood from seventeen to sixty-five years old, middle age from sixty-five to seventy-nine years old, and old age from seventy-nine to ninety-nine years old; beyond a hundred years old is considered extremely old age. These guidelines seem to reflect our reality much better than our old perception of the forties as the beginning of middle age and sixties as the beginning of old age. In my experience, they hold true. I became the head of my family at eighteen when my father passed away and I started working and worked until sixty-five when I retired as a teaching doctor, so I'd say my adulthood stretched across that exact period. And what about middle age—from sixty-five to seventy-nine? That's when I finally became truly independent and could dedicate my time and resources to the kind of work I found meaningful. So it seems to line up.

I began to contemplate postretirement life long before my actual retirement. I was inspired by Kim Hong Ho, a fellow professor at Ewha University Hospital. On the day of his own retirement, he announced: "Today I've become a student again." This unique farewell stuck with me, and I realized that retirement could be another beginning rather than an end. Right there and then, I decided to see my own retirement as a starting point rather than a finish line too.

My life before retirement always felt like a balancing act: trying to solve a long equation full of variables. As father, scholar, doctor, husband, teacher, and son, I had the seemingly impossible mission of juggling all these roles that required different responsibilities and navigating all the conflicting and digressive desires without disrupting fragile harmony. More often than not, I compromised my conflicting desires and prioritized what had to be done. But then my kids were all grown up, and retirement from my teaching position was right around the corner. So suddenly, at the age of sixty-five, I had a lot of free time on my hands for the first time. No one was going to stand in my way now.

What did I want to do with all this time? I gave it a lot of thought and finally decided that I wanted to make use of my experience and knowledge for as many people as possible. That's how I opened my clinic. I introduced experimental treatments such as art therapy and meditation-based psychotherapy. And then I founded the Family Academia Foundation.

In following my psychiatric patients' stories, I often discovered the presence of an ailing family member along the way. My sociologist wife and I decided to help people understand the roles and importance of family. Our foundation grew into a research center that specializes in family-related studies, consulting education, re-education of senior citizens, and parenting coaching.

Another thing that enriched my postretirement life—something I started purely for fun—was enrolling in a four-year cultural studies program at The Cyber University of Korea. Even when I was a medical practitioner, I always had this insatiable desire to study humanities in more depth. I always felt understanding each mental patient called for a much broader and interdisciplinary perspective than an analysis of circumstances unique to the patient. I often felt a need to look carefully into the patient's culture, immediate and broader environments, and communities. I admit that this probably had something to do with my fascination with Nepalese culture, especially its spiritual aspects. I wanted to discover what it was about culture that's so irresistible to me. By a twist of fate, I came across a poster calling for new students for the cyber university program and jumped at the opportunity. I finally had a chance to satiate my thirst for cultural studies!

And this was by far the most fun I've had studying in my whole life. No pressure about getting good grades, no worries about the tests; I only studied out of my academic curiosity, and I couldn't think of more fun in this world. So it happened that in 2011, I graduated from the program first in class and as the oldest student. In all of my years as a student, in youth, I never even came close to this kind of honor, and to achieve this feat at the age of seventy-six? Life sure is full of surprises.

The opening of my clinic, the establishment of the Family Academia Foundation, and the cyber university years—all this might sound like an old man bragging about "how I lived my life to the fullest." But no, what I'm telling you, reader, is that all this has happened at a slow pace, over the course of twenty long years. We think of our postretirement life as "the rest of our life." The rest, which is to say, what remains, some left-overs. But the time we get to live after retirement can often be too long to be considered mere scraps. Twenty years—that's enough time for a child to be born and grow up to be an adult. That's enough time for you to start something new and set it on the right course. My reader, it's a long, long time—way too long for you to spend sitting around and sticking with the same old, same old, without taking on some exciting new challenges.

Some people consider postretirement life a period in which they'll be rendered useless. They can barely face their old age, fearing they may become a nuisance and burden to their family and society, without careers or health to speak of. They strive to prove their worth. But happiness will always stay out of reach, no matter how wealthy and altruistic they may be, unless they change their own points of view on life and stop thinking of themselves in old age as potential problems for everyone.

Ellen Langer, an esteemed psychology professor at Harvard, said that the last thing we should give up, if we were looking to be happy, is control over our lives—the right to make our own decisions in life. What's the best thing about aging? My answer will always be the same: it's the freedom that comes with having your life under control. You're no longer locked down by all your responsibilities and you have enough experience and resources to commit to the kind of work that you've always wanted. This freedom is a reward for those who have lived their lives to the best of their abilities, so why waste it weighing your options and not taking action instead of finally following your heart?

I always say, "Now is my golden age." How different do you think a newborn's one year is from an old man's one year? What about a twenty-something's day from an eighty-something's? All of us are equal in that time doesn't wait for any of us. That's why you must keep your mind open, no matter how old or young you are.

Let's forget terms like the "rest of your life" or "remaining days," because your life after retirement can and should amount to much more than that. When you own your life and spend every day pursuing what your heart truly desires, you won't be disappointed. It'll be a hell of a ride. Anna Mary Robertson Moses, who first tried her hand at painting at seventy-five years old and left around 1,600 paintings when she died at one hundred and one, said: "Life is what we make it, always has been, always will be."

2

THERE'S NO BETTER TIME TO GET CLOSER TO YOUR FAMILY

I'VE BEEN INVITED TO speak at many events since the publication of my writing in Korea in 2013. I've done a lot of interviews and lectures and been a guest on a number of TV shows, through which I've connected with a lot of people, and been socially and professionally active—what a good fortune in old age! And whatever the occasion, everyone seemed to have one question in common. People always want to hear about our family's lifestyle: how we, thirteen people from three generations, live under the same roof.

As I briefly mentioned in an earlier chapter, I live in a villa in Gugi-dong, Seoul. Five families live in this four-story villa, and all of the residents are my sons and daughters, and their spouses and children. But don't jump to the conclusion that I was rich enough to give each of my children a unit. Each unit was bought and mortgaged by each of them, without my help.

We've been living together in this villa since 2002, a year when all of my children were going through a hectic phase of life, married with kids and working full-time jobs. My eldest son suggested that we all chip in to solve this dilemma of raising children and taking care of aging parents, while paying for housing in the expensive capital city of South Korea. We were all immediately enthusiastic, but we couldn't easily decide how to make this plan a reality. We were aware that there would be challenges for our extended family—of aging parents and grown-up children and their own children—to live peacefully together. What if we ran into conflict after conflict and the family ended up torn apart rather than brought closer together? But after much discussion, our family decided to live together under the guiding principle of "respect for the independence of each family and every family member."

Even from the early stage of building the villa, we followed this principle. My wife and I provided the lot our original house was built on, and my children took into their own hands the matters of designing each of the units suitable for their budget, tastes, and family needs. We made sure to build a separate entry for each unit, for privacy. These principles of respect and independence also apply to our day-to-day etiquette. It's strictly prohibited for anyone to enter another family's unit or call someone out without a prior appointment; the passcode to each unit is only known by the family that occupies it. Each of us takes turns hosting and planning family events—the duty lasting for six months each time—with dates and places always announced in advance.

Nowadays, we're past the age of nuclear families and heading into the era of one-person families, and so, naturally, many people find our intergenerational home refreshing. They like to call it a "new family experiment" or "new form of community." They often enviously tell us that this form of family—independent while virtually living under the same roof—is the ideal twenty-first-century family model, and fantasize about family meals and lots of quality time on a day-to-day basis. It looks to me that many people consider our family model to be perfect.

But we're all human. We're not always gleefully laughing at each other's jokes and having the time of our life together. In fact, we might seem on the verge of indifference toward one another at times. Even though we live in the same villa, sometimes days go by without us seeing each other, and everyone is so busy we're not up-to-speed on each other's lives. But this touch of indifference may just be the secret ingredient to our consistent harmony. I'm afraid you'll be disappointed if you expected a portrait of a more intimate, emotionally interdependent family.

Speaking from experience, though, the true upside of a big, intergenerational family becomes clearer in times of hardship than of joy.

Back in 2010, my eldest son collapsed on a Sunday evening. His wife and daughter were by his side when it happened. Since he didn't have any preexisting health conditions, his wife thought he was just pulling her leg, but my eldest granddaughter had just heard of her friend's father recently dying of a heart attack, and called for an ambulance right away. And then she called her aunt—my eldest daughter—who's a medical doctor and who advised her to rush her father to the hospital immediately. My younger son was thankfully at home—just downstairs—that day, so he drove them to the hospital himself rather than wait for an ambulance. And it was a far faster first aid response than an ambulance could have provided.

With odds in their favor, they found the emergency department fully staffed that day, with all of the doctors there for a medical team evaluation, including the chief surgeon. So my son got the necessary medical care the moment he arrived in the hospital and was immediately moved to the operating table.

It turned out my son had a case of myocardial infarction. When he arrived at the hospital, half of his cardiac muscle had already died. If he'd only gotten there a few minutes later, he could have had irreversible brain damage or even died. Since my family lived in the same villa, they could put their heads together and handle the crisis quickly and wisely. I don't know what would have happened had it not been for the quick wit of my granddaughter, the advice of my daughter, and my younger son's ride to the ER. What if even a single one of these ingredients had been missing? My family's "collective intelligence" saved my son's life. That moment, I felt deep in my bones that it was the right decision to live together as an intergenerational family.

While he and his wife were in the hospital, my wife, my other children, and I looked after his daughter and took care of the housework. His daughter—my granddaughter—didn't take her father's condition too badly thanks to the rest of the family that happily stepped in and was there for her when she needed support. My granddaughter brings it up even now. Recently she told me, "The best thing you've ever done? Definitely how you brought us all together to live in this villa." And I wholeheartedly agree.

For over two decades now my family has lived together, each going through many little and big challenges along the way. And we have all relied on each other in times of need. To share life's risks and wisely handle crises—that's the true gift of having a big, intergenerational family. Society may seem to have made slow and sure progress in shrinking the list of life's possible risks, but is that really the case? Our life expectancy might be longer with medical advances, but that also means we're to spend year after year coping with various diseases when we're older. Modern society endorses women's career advancement, but pays little attention to the issue of how working families find the time and resources to rear children. Higher education no longer means better jobs. Our modern society's progress birthed unexpected, complicated problems, and its individualistic culture also leaves us dealing with them largely by ourselves. But can these problems really be solved without help?

Behind the decision for our multigenerational family of thirteen to live together was the pressing, realistic need to solve these difficult problems with each other's help. To share the burden of all these risks and have a social safety net. In terms of the issue of looking after aging parents alone, once we started living in the same villa, it meant that my children could have free weekends without worrying about me and my wife. Once we were living next door and could check on each other whenever we needed to, we no longer felt the need to go out of our ways to set a date and meet up on a regular basis. We could all relax on the weekends, which also helped us get along. My children got the help they desperately needed in raising their kids. My wife took over the task of getting our grandchildren to school. And with eight adult relatives in the villa, there was always at least one person who could babysit if necessary. This allowed my children to relax and focus on their careers. And my grandchildren had a lot of good influence from their older relatives. From astronomer and medical doctor to art therapist and experimental film director, adults working in various fields offered stimulating, new experiences to these little kids and helped expand their horizons. Nowadays, most people raise two children at most, so always having their cousins around gives my grandchildren more chances to socialize and learn how to get along with people.

Of course, living so close to your family won't all be smooth sailing. A shortcut to the peaceful coexistence of aging parents and their grown-up children lies in allowing each other to take care of themselves when they can. I believe every family thrives in the soil softened by just the right amount of benign indifference. But what if your family comes across an obstacle they need your help with? Now that's the moment when you need to step in. Today, there's a growing movement to build a small town-level community, just as in the old days when a whole Korean village often shared in looking after the village kids, and to cultivate a culture of communal parenting. I'd encourage anyone who is able to, to try this idea of communal parenting with their own extended family.

Don't feel the pressure to ask nothing of your family, because you feel that's the way it's supposed to be. Remember that, in this unpredictable society, your family is a dependable safety net. They're the ones you can always fall back on. Count your family's communal knowledge and labor as one of your most important assets. Once you decide to leverage these valuable assets, you'll find numerous ways to do so, which will help you better tackle life's curveballs. And if your family becomes closer in the process, that's an added blessing.

3

THE FUTURE BEGINS WITH
THE NEXT GENERATION

A WHILE AGO, MY acquaintance broached this rather carefully: "Your eldest son says he'll forgo *jesa* altogether once you're gone, did you know?"

He'd probably seen and become concerned over my son's Facebook post declaring his intention to abandon the *jesa* tradition altogether after my passing. In old age, my acquaintance said, we should work to remain close with our children, and he also went on to advise me to keep my son in his place. I just laughed it off, joking I'd be one hungry soul then! Well, I've always known about my son's dislike for this Korean tradition. In honoring the tradition of *jesa*, Korean families prepare feasts for their dead ancestors on the anniversaries of their deaths each year, according to the now obsolete lunar calendar. Traditionally, each feast consists of at least ten dishes, all freshly made by the female members of the family once everyone gathers at the home of the eldest living son. In fact, my son abhors all kinds of formalities, so it's really no surprise that he can't wait to get rid of this traditional ritual for the dead.

Long story short, my reader, I hold no grudge against my son. My family history, in fact, points to generations of daring adaptations and progressive thinking when it comes to matters of *jesa*. My family's *sunsan* (선산: a mountain passed down generations in Korean families for the burial of all their family members) used to hold six different burial sites managed by a ranger. In the middle of the Korean War, however, our *sunsan* became a shanty town for refugees as everyone was fleeing Northern provinces. Soon the high school building nearby also became a temporary hospital to accommodate injured soldiers, forcing the school to make use of parts of our *sunsan* as space for gym classes. During this time, we could even enjoy the unusual scene of a teacher trying to give the students a lesson on top of a tomb.

So, it was obviously time to move our burial sites, but my father and his nine siblings had trouble agreeing on how to proceed. My mother, as they were in a deadlock, came up with the idea of cremating everyone and scattering the ashes along the Nakdong River. The sheer audacity of her suggestion was scandalous for the time. It couldn't have been easy, of course, for her to voice her opinion—with six female in-laws and two male in-laws present, who, all being older, had more authority in the traditional Korean family. But my mother managed to persuade every single one of them, basing her argument on the fact that my father, the eldest son, was ill and pointing out the obvious difficulty of managing the burial sites. In the end, my mother took charge of all of the *pamyo* (파묘: the act of unearthing graves and moving the bodies buried in them) and cremation process, with the help of just one worker, which signals that her argument, though accepted, likely wasn't embraced with enough enthusiasm to mobilize family volunteers. But my mother chose pragmatism and change over traditions that everyone would have surely struggled to keep up with.

When I was sixteen and my father passed away, I became the head of the family based on the Korean laws of that time.

One of the first decisions I made was to switch to the solar calendar for all *jesa* dates and announced to my entire extended family that we would no longer honor this tradition for our numerous ancestors, but instead would focus on two former generations—which meant our parents' and grandparents' generations. My aunts couldn't believe their ears when I first brought this up, and even showed up with food and props on lunar dates instead of solar dates a few times. This would catch me off guard each time since I had stopped following the lunar calendar, which had been outdated since before my birth. But I stood my ground and kept persuading them, explaining it was all because I wouldn't be able to keep track of the lunar dates once all of my older relatives fluent in these matters were gone, and finally, my family, one by one, gave in. We've been honoring this Korean tradition according to the solar calendar ever since, thank goodness.

When all of my older relatives had passed away, I felt once again it was time for change. This was around 2002, back when my wife and I started to live together with our children in our communal villa. My family had quite the discussion on *jesa*. And I decided only to celebrate the *jesa* dates of my own parents and pay respects to the older generations during two major Korean holidays—Lunar New Year and Korean Thanksgiving—instead of their actual *jesa* dates. I also suggested that, if we were not to be trained to follow this tradition word for word, we should rethink its overall format so it'd better fit our reality. My entire family sat around the table and had a heated debate. As a result, we ended up with two principles. First, our *jesa* will always be a potluck. Second, all family members will honor this tradition in accordance with their respective religious beliefs. For the last fourteen years, my family has been honoring this old Korean tradition without the usual conflicts many Korean families still go through, over how much food they should prepare, when they celebrate, and how many generations and times a year.

You see, I'm a doctor. Which is to say, I'm a believer in science. I must confess that I have no faith in the unproven existence of the afterlife or my ancestors' hungry spirits hovering over me on the dates of their deaths, expecting a feast. So *jesa* doesn't really mean an annual ritual for the dead to me, after all. It has come to mean a time when we—the living—can honor the dead and learn to embrace their absence. So it should be a meaningful, memorable time for the living. If the living are to fight over the details of this ritual every year and grow apart—forgive me for saying this—that tradition has already become meaningless and it's better to let it die out. And why not adapt a ritual for the dead to the reality of the living? Based on these beliefs, I've kept trying to find the right way to honor this tradition.

But now, my son's taking a step further and proclaiming that he will stop following this tradition altogether. This means that he'll make the decision as the eldest and leader of the family, once I'm gone, to bid farewell to the tradition that calls for so much sacrifice and labor from all of our family members. It's just as my mother decided to cremate all of our ancestors' bodies, just as I downsized and simplified the *jesa* ritual significantly—it's a proclamation of respect for the next, younger generation in the family and their needs, and a nod to modernization. Some people might find this unacceptable, of course, and tut away at our ruination of this old tradition, but I'm all for change! My reader, I clearly see that my time has passed and welcome my son's generation being in charge from here on out.

And really, after my death, the matter of this tradition, just like everything else, is entirely up to my children. My children taking charge and making changes for the future does nothing but take some of the load off my shoulders. Now it's time for me to leave decisions for the family to my children and spend the rest of my life focusing on myself and my wellbeing. How liberating!

My reader, don't take it personally when the time comes for your children to lead your family. The bigger problem, you might be forgetting, is when your children refuse to take charge and have no interest in bringing the family together without your involvement; that forces you to spend your precious time in old age worrying over and taking care of small and big family matters. And your children, as you do, will also have to delegate all important decisions to you and wait for you to make up your mind every time. And what a waste of time! In this vicious cycle, old parents become overbearing, and grown-up children lose confidence in the family dynamic. It's already hard to cultivate and maintain a strong bond with your children in old age, and this mistake will only make it worse.

Of course, I understand, as a parent, that your children might not quite live up to your expectations. Especially, if you yourself have made great accomplishments in life, you might all too easily fall into the trap of doubting and underestimating your children every step of their way. But you should learn to respect your children for who they are once they're grown up. Even if they sometimes make mistakes in your eyes, you should let them learn from those mistakes in their own ways. You've done a great job of raising your children until now—you've fed, clothed and educated them, haven't you? Now it's time to take a step back and accept that your job of parenting is done. Learn to become, instead, their best supporter and cheerleader, no matter what path they choose in life. Remember that your children cannot grow well in that long shadow you cast, if you don't step aside and let the sun in.

Every parent's final goal is the true independence of their children. But no one can become fully independent on the first try. Just as it takes a toddler falling thousands of times to learn to stand and start walking upright, all children become gradually independent, through trial and error. Falling and failing are the first to come before standing upright, way before walking upright; likewise, your children do not suddenly become independent but learn to, as they try and fail. Allow your children to stand on their own first, so they can start making their own decisions. In whichever age, a future always began when the new generation, necessarily and inevitably, outgrew the older generation.

4

YOU ARE, QUITE LITERALLY,
A LIVING MIRACLE

IN 2011, MY WIFE and I went on a two-day-long couples' retreat to Jeju Island with my fellow medical school alumni and their spouses to celebrate the fiftieth anniversary of our graduation. The last day of our retreat was Sunday, so some of my religious friends went to church. In the afternoon, my Catholic friends returned, fuming. Something the priest said had really upset them.

The priest asked them, a group of unfamiliar worshippers, what brought them all the way from the mainland, what the special occasion was. They answered that they were on a trip for the fiftieth anniversary of their med school graduation, to which the priest said, "Oh, what a long life!"

My friends were outraged and couldn't stop grinding their teeth even back at the hotel. They criticized the priest with bad-tempered comments like "How dare he treat us like oldies" and "He was basically asking why we're not dead yet."

I, for one, still don't believe the priest meant any harm. It's more likely that my friends, who had a hard time accepting their aging selves, interpreted the priest's comment in the worst way possible. I tried to calm them down, saying, "The priest must have meant to congratulate you on making it through all the hardships, so don't take it personally."

In fact, most people of my generation, including me, have just barely made it through the past century. Our everyday lives were under constant threats of poverty, disease, and war. At six years old, I had a bad case of typhoid fever. We didn't have a way to treat it then, so all I could do was pray for my dear life. Fortunately, I came out of the fever alive. Near the end of Japanese colonial rule, I was nine and was exempt from Japan's draft calls for the junior air force since I was just one year short. But all around me, ten-, eleven-, twelve-year-old boys got drafted as kamikaze trainees (suicide squad). When I was fourteen, during the Korean War, we were in the middle of a crisis, on the verge of losing the Nakdong River front line, and the Korean military would conduct nighttime searches to find more soldiers. I wasn't drafted, however, since I wasn't of age—again by one year—and instead found myself working alongside a combat artist and assisting in the production of war propaganda posters. Later, I found myself right in the midst of Korean history's torrents during the times of the April Revolution and Gwangju Uprising, but managed to survive through all that till now—if that wasn't some divine intervention, I don't know what is.

One of my cousins was accused of being a communist sympathizer and subsequently killed in the massacre that took place in Geochang Valley, Daegu. His younger son died in the army during the Korean War. My youngest uncle died in the war as well, and my second uncle was abducted by the North Korean army. If you ask Korean people my age, they will have similar stories of suffering. Death and great loss always hovered nearby, so life itself felt like a miracle. I often say, "You might think anyone can have eighty years of life, but not everyone will."

Whenever I talk about the universe with my son, the astronomer, I'm at a loss for words in the face of its sheer immensity. This planet that we call home came into existence by pure chance, in this boundless universe that stretches far beyond our grasp; our entire human race has existed for only a small modicum of time in the entire history of the earth—4.6 billion years. I, Rhee Kun Hoo, am the tiniest dust flake that'll float for a moment and disappear, in the grand scheme of things. Wouldn't you say the existence of any one of us is a miracle in and of itself?

In my youth, I brimmed with confidence and determination, sure I would make my own way in life. Sometimes my hard work was rewarded, and sometimes it wasn't, and yet I always held none but myself accountable for my success and failure. All in all, this life of such faith has been both joyful and fulfilling. But in retrospect, I see that my life has been driven by the forces of great coincidence and many chance encounters. The power of coincidence and chance encounters has thankfully been in my favor, and so here I am, still breathing.

Don't take things in your life for granted. Life with relative health itself is not a privilege everyone gets to enjoy, and is not simply a reward for your hard work alone, either. In this interdependent, close-knit world, no one stands alone. Knowingly or unknowingly, we always influence each other. When you understand your place in the grand scheme of things, you cannot help but feel humbled and grateful. And someone who's lived long enough to have been so humbled can be a great influence on another life.

5

Every Day Can Be a Celebration

In 2014, I turned eighty years old in Korean age. Until 2023, Koreans had a unique way of counting age. We were all considered one year old upon birth, and everyone simultaneously gained one year when a new calendar year began, regardless of individual birthdays. Eighty years, in my opinion, is the mark of old age, and I was no exception. Sleepy eyelids, white hair, bad hearing and eyesight, a slow gait, and slouchy shoulders—all unmistakably elderly. I thought: No one would hesitate to call me Grandpa now.

One day I was climbing an overpass on my way to my office, and a middle-aged man walking by greeted me in passing, "You look great, Pops." I just returned a quiet smile. What season in life was the man himself passing through? Maybe the season for grave responsibility and duty, that could be overwhelming and rewarding all at the same time. Yes, an early autumn, a time for ripening fruits once the scalding sun and stormy weather's all behind you.

Now I'm past the scorching summer, past the fruitful autumn, and have reached this winter of serenity. With all my achievements and glory in the past, all my anger and resentment no longer thorns in my side, I'm at long last free and at peace with the world. My eighties might just be the golden peak of old age.

And how could I possibly share all this joy I've found in my eighties with people I care about? With my eightieth birthday fast approaching, I had a lot on my mind. I wanted to curate some meaningful event for this birthday and share some memorable moments with people in my life I'm grateful for.

"This year, every day will be my birthday," I announced to my family when they asked me what I wanted for my birthday. Eighty years is too long a time to celebrate in just one day, I decided. And if I gathered all of my relatives and friends in one place and shared one expensive meal but wouldn't even get to talk to each of them in a meaningful way, what good would that do? So I wanted to take a year to meet all of my dear ones in person, one by one, thank each of them personally over a delicious meal, and look back on my life.

But of course, hitting up someone out of the blue for my eightieth birthday celebration would put too much pressure on the person. So I made appointments without mentioning my birthday. And only after we'd had a wonderful time over a nice meal, when we were about to part, did I reveal to them that it was my eightieth birthday.

I mostly got two reactions. The first was an apologetic response that they would have treated me to a nicer meal had they known beforehand. But every meal was more than nice enough for any birthday of mine. The second was an appreciation for this unique idea of celebrating one's birthday all year round. For your eightieth birthday, your family tends to plan something grand and spend a lot, but on the actual day, you usually end up feeling too overwhelmed to enjoy the event itself. The friends I met for my eightieth birthday told me they would also have to rethink what they wanted to do with their upcoming eightieth birthdays.

Every Day Can Be a Celebration

How many times in life do you think you become the star of a party, of a big celebration? Your first birthday, wedding, sixtieth, seventieth, and eightieth birthdays . . . all of which still won't amount to ten times in a lifetime. And such an occasion is one of the rare opportunities for your loved ones to gather in one place to celebrate you, but too hung up on propriety and event details, we miss out too often on the pleasure of celebrating and being celebrated. Yes, everything might be glittery on the surface, but take a closer look, and we see how such a day can often be a glimpse of utter chaos. Who could that kind of party really celebrate, apart from the owner of the buffet where your event took place?

Remember the question I get most often from my readers is "How come you managed to have so much fun?" And my answer: "When did I ever say I *had* fun? I said I *want to* have fun." Life is made up, in large part, of ordinary days rather than memorable delights or extreme sorrows. If you continue to find fault with ordinary days, therefore, you'll naturally end up spending most of your life discontented and bored, but if you seek out whatever joy and fun you can in those mundane days, your life, as the total sum, will be a hell of a lot of fun. That's my secret to a happy life—seeking out whatever joy and fun I can in my everyday life. And a celebratory day is one of the best opportunities for you to have a lot of fun. I mean, it's a day when people are already keen to celebrate you, so why not make the best of that opportunity and get celebrated the way you want? How much fun would that be?

I visited an exhibit on Jeju Island, hosted by an artist whose primary medium was East Asian paintings—also a member of Family Academia—in celebration of his sixtieth birthday. Looking around the exhibition, I stumbled upon a portrait of someone that looked oddly familiar. On closer examination, I realized the painting was of my smiling face!

The artist caught the look on my face, and told me with a smile: "I've painted the faces of sixty of the most memorable people in my life from the last sixty years. I was so happy working on this painting. It's based on a snapshot taken that day we volunteered at the orphanage together."

His words and painting were such a heartwarming gift— and I thought I was the one there to celebrate him! The generosity to turn his own birthday into a chance to thank others surely reflected who he was—always gentle, considerate, and lighting up everyone around him.

Just because nothing special seems to happen to you, you shouldn't go through life bored and disinterested. You can find fun anywhere. The passive attitude with which you face the world is often the very reason why you end up dissatisfied. You should actively seek out fun—that's the only way to make it happen.

My real eightieth birthday—the Korean one—was December 30, 2014. On this actual eightieth birthday of mine, my family of thirteen threw a small party for ourselves. My children went to a fish market at sunrise to get top-notch sashimi, which I love, and we had a small banquet of sashimi and a fish stew made of the leftovers and fishbones. Then followed the conventional Korean gift of money. We had a brief moment to share some memories from eighty years of my life. It was perfect in every way, so satisfying and casual, and no fancy event could have celebrated my last eighty years better.

6

THE FREEDOM TO FIND YOUR OWN VALUES

NOWADAYS, WHEN I'M WATCHING TV or on the internet, I come across so many words that I find hard to understand, usually acronyms. I'm sure for the younger generations it's all a piece of cake, but we older folks find these words intimidating. And you can't really avoid learning these words either, since there are just so many of them now, and they're widely used; these acronyms have become essential for smooth conversations. Sometimes I feel like a clueless anime character, blinking at every word.

At first, I needed my grandchildren's help even with the most rudimentary ones like ㅋㅋ (lmao) or ㅎㅎ (lol), but man, have things escalated in these past few decades! Now it's on another level. So, I launched my independent studies to master these coined words and acronyms, asking for help from my grandchildren if needed and researching on my own. *Gapbunssa* (갑분싸) means it's become awkward all of a sudden. They call the men who gave up on starting a family or looking after the existing one *gaponam* (가포남) and women who have made the same choices *gaponyeo* (가포녀). These acronyms speak volumes about our Korean society where you can't survive in any corporate environment unless you give up on family. Those who know their manners are called *gaetop* (개탑) and the opposites *gaetop-bul* (개탑불). I wrote down these acronyms on eight A4 pages.

Yes, it was an inconvenience, and I was irked for a moment or two, but reading and writing these words was actually pretty fun. One of my favorites, which caught my eye right away, was *sohwakhaeng* (소확행), translated to "small but sure happiness," a trend Korean millennials and Gen Zs live by: sticking with the small but sure happiness they can find in their everyday lives instead of sacrificing their present in pursuit of faraway, uncertain happiness. And this word is a sad reflection of twenty-first-century Korea where what we took for granted once—stability of your job, marriage and starting a family, and owning a place of your own—has become an empty promise.

You know what I really learned from all this? I learned about the sense of betrayal that the younger generations must be feeling toward the world. On the other hand, however, I am proud of them for having pointed out what we—the older generations—haven't had the courage to face. Haven't we mortgaged our present for the sake of our future happiness? So many of us have kept telling ourselves: after I get into college, after I get a stable job, after I get promoted, once I make enough money. Yes, we've been taught to pursue happiness once we're prepared, and so thoroughly and completely prepared, to pursue it. But these younger generations want to live in the moment and grab happiness when it's nearby, and how very wise indeed!

We've all lived such hectic, tunnel-visioned lives in our competitive modern societies. Most of us, I feel, believed in the path of proven success but didn't have the time to question whether or not it was the *right* path for us. On we went, goal-oriented, but one day we found ourselves retired with our kids about to leave the nest, at which point life would surely rock like a mastless ship. Rocking, of course, because you have lost a purpose—the one and only compass in life you know.

The Freedom to Find Your Own Values

If you let yourself get fixated on this feeling of time running out, on top of all this, things will be even worse. And that kind of insecurity will goad you into ambitious projects: you will make it your job to accomplish everything, as if you're still in college pulling an all-nighter. You might become overzealous and try out anything and everything—exercise, travel, volunteer work, studies—whatever it may be that happens to be in vogue. Some people, I've seen, spend a small fortune on a professional-level camera just to try their hands at photography. Some people pay for the most expensive travel packages to finally see the world. Some people brag about their ability to lift weights. Whatever it may be, my reader, some of us surely feel tempted to jump right back into that competitive lifestyle, even when we've retired.

Another surprisingly wonderful thing about aging is that you don't need to set a goal anymore. What are you going to make of all the time you spend studying? You're not getting a PhD now. You can't become an Olympian now even if you work out all the time. Travel around and brag about it, sure, but you'll find it difficult to land a willing audience. So why would we, in our old age, study, work out, and travel? I'd say do it for pure fun. Not because we have a goal or are trying to make something out of it, but because we take pleasure in the process of doing it.

From goal to process, from extrinsic motivation to self-motivation. This is the transformation of life you'll need to go through in old age, sooner or later. Life is longer than you think, and will only get longer from here on out. If you're to cross this long river of old age, you need something better than a lifeboat made of other people's values. You need a sturdy, reliable one made of your own. What do you like, what inspires you, and what gives meaning to your life? Why don't you find these out first?

Years ago, I watched an interesting documentary called *A Hundred Years Old: Shock* (100세 쇼크). A middle-aged woman said in one interview that she'd begun to wonder what she truly enjoyed in life a while ago, and went on to say: "I love meaningful work and volunteering, but more than anything, I want to feel full of life, from deep within." Eventually, she chose philosophy as her area of focus. She radiated with happiness as she said she'd never imagined studying philosophy at her age could be so much fun.

I meet a lot of people depressed about the loss of their life goals. But is there any answer to life other than living and being true to yourself? Every goal is a placeholder except for finding and becoming your true self. Now is the time for you to think about this bigger question of life: What do you truly desire? The answer to this question is the key to your happiness.

7

THE PURE JOY OF DOING SOMETHING FOR THE HECK OF IT

IN 1996, I RECEIVED from the Association of Korean Writers a rather strange prize called "The Most Literary Award." It's a prize for someone who's not a literary writer but feels very much like one. Anyway, I was elated. It was as if my long, unrequited love for poetry had been officially acknowledged at last.

There's a good reason why I describe my love for poetry as *unrequited*. I'm second to none when it comes to a love for poetry, but I'm not gifted at all in the art of poetry writing itself. When I was nine years old, Korea finally became an independent country, and I learned the Korean language for the first time. My teacher was ecstatic and wanted to spread the joy of Korean independence, and so took us students to a park for an outdoor class. We were assigned two hours of free writing. Back then, I was going through a rough patch and a bit of an identity crisis due to all the social transitions following Korea's independence. Naturally, I had my head in the clouds a lot, and even during this writing class, I had way too much on my mind. Daydreaming, I suddenly heard my teacher announce, "Everyone, time to wrap up!" Two hours had passed in the blink of an eye. Panicked, I wrote down on my notepad, in Korean: "I came to this park for a writing class."

Ridiculous, I know, but this is the first sentence I ever wrote in Korean. You get the idea—I'm no poet, and never will be.

It wasn't that different in high school. Near the end of the Korean War, I heard the news of a pro-democracy demonstration erupting in Budapest, Hungary's capital city. So deeply moved by this outcry for democracy in a Communist country, not to mention one of the Soviet Union's satellite states, I wrote a poem and submitted it to my literature teacher. I remember it being about the importance of freedom. But the teacher, who also happened to be a poet, called me aside later and told me: "I have no idea what you're trying to say."

Sure, a good poet needs the right sensibility (which I felt I had), but they must also have an eye for words and verse form. But my poem disregarded word and form alike. So of course, it couldn't convey my sentiment, and so my love went unrequited.

In college, I even founded an association of aspiring student poets, and got a professor involved in training us. But writing poetry remained out of reach. With much regret, I gave up on becoming a poet. And yet I remained a poetry lover my whole life.

But this prize—The Most Literary Award—rekindled my love for poetry. I recruited a group of acquaintances who loved poetry as much as I did and started what we called "Yeti Poetry Recital Club." Club members meet on the second Thursday evening of every month and everyone recites poems—some of their favorites or their own—then we have a discussion after. And once a month, we go to the Gwangmyeong Orphanage to spend sometime with the kids there. The club has just celebrated its twentieth anniversary.

Some of our members are published poets, but most of them are ordinary office workers. Which is to say, those in one-sided love affairs with poetry, just like me. This sense of belonging is probably why I always feel right at home in any of our club meetings. Listening to our members read their own poems brings me such a sense of peace, and reading my poetry out loud in front of the club makes me feel as if I have indeed become a poet. Yeti Club has always been a place where I could decompress and cultivate my waning poetic sensibility. And I cherish, beyond what I can express in words, this monthly opportunity to become a poet.

In the world of work, what you're good at overshadows what you want to do. Because, fundamentally, professionals compete. It's a plus if you love your job, but the more important merit is your competence. That's just the way it works. But competition entails stress, of course. And from high expectations comes pressure. It's the same even if you manage to get your dream job, because it is still a job, after all. So we need something we can purely enjoy and indulge, without competition, without a constant need for improvement, that helps us decompress. That's why we need an avocation—a hobby outside of work.

Take a moment to look back on your life. How competitive has it been? From all those years in school when you competed for good grades to get into a good college, to all your work to get a good job, to get ahead—so much competition. Having competed for everything our whole lives, we instinctively try to be good at our hobbies too. But it's impossible to be good at everything. You just need to be good at your job. The rest you need only to enjoy and do just as much as you want, too. I'm no good at poetry, but I've been enjoying it for twenty years with no problem at all. Experience for yourself the simple act of doing what you enjoy, without the pressure of competition, and see just how much it enriches your life.

Nowadays, I'm into two hobbies. The first one is listening to lectures at Galdar, a bookshop that specializes in scientific reference texts. This independent bookshop was founded by my eldest son—the astronomer—and his science-loving friends, and I became a shareholder. It's a wonderful project: a place to sell science books and host lectures on scientific discoveries. Every time I'm in the audience for one of these lectures, I'm at a loss for words at the profound mysteries of the universe. Learning something new gives me immense pleasure, even though someone might wonder what I'm going to do with all this newly acquired knowledge in my eighties. But so what if I don't make anything out of all this knowledge? Now that I'm this old, I should be free to explore whatever gives me pleasure, without worrying about putting it to use.

Another one is a stamp club. I've been collecting quite a lot of stamps ever since I started traveling to Nepal. One day, I sorted through my collection, which, I realized, amounted to a considerable size. What am I to do with my collection? After much online surfing, I found an online community called "The Association of Stamp Lovers." As soon as I became a member, I started running fun quizzes with prizes of Nepalese stamps for the winners. Only several months in, I became the most popular member. Though I started out as a total novice, over the course of two years, I learned a huge amount about stamps as a member of this association. Based on this experience, I put together three books about Nepalese stamps, for one of which I won a prize at the 2018 Asian International Stamp Exhibition in Bangkok, in the category of philatelic (stamp-related) literature. All this recognition and publication for a hobby I picked up to have some fun in old age—what a windfall!

As you age, your professional world naturally decreases in scale. If you're one of those who have only sought a sense of purpose in work, you might wind up going through a huge identity crisis after retirement, or even feeling utterly useless. But retirement doesn't mean the end of the world. In order to feel grounded in your postretirement life, you should learn to build and have in place a world of versatile hobbies. Of course, the earlier you start, the better. But it's never too late to get into a new hobby, even close to retirement. I started a new hobby in my eighties. Remember there's zero pressure, so long as you enjoy it. Don't brush this advice off. I want you to share in the life-enriching delight of doing what you love just for the heck of it.

PART 5

HOW TO START YOUR HAPPILY EVER AFTER TODAY

1

Make Peace with the Inevitable Guest

When he was in his twenties, my grandson once asked me, "Grandpa, when you're at your age, what's on your mind? I was always curious. You know, I've still got a long way to go till I'm as old as you."

I gave it a little thought and answered: "Huh, you're curious about that? Truth is, I always have death on my mind."

My grandson looked startled. He probably didn't expect this kind of answer, having seen how I was going about my everyday life with so much energy and optimism.

"You're afraid of death, Grandpa?"

"Oh, of course. After all, no one can tell me what it's like. Not knowing makes us afraid. But of course, I won't become immortal, afraid or not. All lives must come to an end. So I try to live every single day to the fullest and not forget to be grateful."

My grandson tilted his head, pensive. He probably didn't understand it, not really. When I was a young man, I also didn't feel the chilling inevitability in matters of life and death, at least not the way I do now. Reader, each of us needs to experience a life-altering event or live many years to start taking these matters truly seriously.

As I mentioned in an earlier chapter, my father passed away at forty-nine. I was in high school at the time. After his passing, I began to feel an irrational yet potent fear of death always gnawing at the pit of my stomach. I was afraid I wouldn't outlive my father. It took me a long time to finally confront this fear of mine, because I kept pushing it to the back of my mind and had been in denial. When I visited the Himalayas for the first time I was forty-nine, the age my father had been when he passed away. I was selected to join this expedition as a member of a scholarly organization, but even after the organization's time there, I chose to stay behind for six more months, trekking all over Nepal. During this time, I also climbed a mountain 5,000 meters above sea level with a Sherpa, carrying a tent and nothing else. It was there that I confronted the fear I'd been avoiding all along: my fear of death. How vulnerable I was, a fragile human being ascending the Himalayas. One misstep or an unexpected shift in the weather could unintentionally end my life on that ruthless mountain. Once I came face-to-face with my fear of death, it became an important philosophical axis for my life.

Let me take you back to a time when I felt death breathing down my neck. It was in 2003, when I went to Nepal on a medical volunteer trip, and suddenly I wasn't able to see through one of my eyes. It was probably because of the drastic altitude and climate change during my hike, or all the stress associated with looking after my volunteer group, but it turned out the blood vessels in my eye had burst. Upon returning to South Korea, I underwent emergency surgery at a university hospital, but my eyesight didn't recover. During the operation, doctors discovered the congenital narrowing of the blood vessels in my heart. The situation was so urgent that I was immediately scheduled for another surgery. This procedure involved taking an artery from my arm and transplanting it into my heart's blood vessels—an extremely complex and challenging task. It was quite literally a fifty-fifty chance between life and death. That's when I decided: If I survived this big surgery, I would consider the rest of my life a bonus. I would not let it be plagued by regrets or greed.

Thankfully, the surgery was a success, and when I came to, my heart filled with immense joy at my second chance at life. Ever since the surgery, every single day, I now wake up with this first elated thought: What a miracle that I am granted another day, that I haven't died overnight! I've learned to appreciate life in all its glorious ordinariness. This is not to say I have by any means conquered my fear of death, but I'm no longer allowing that fear to control me.

Twelve years later, in 2015, I once again confronted the very real possibility of death when I slipped on my way down from my unit in the villa and fell, landing hard on my head. Lying on the cold concrete, I touched my trembling hand to my head, which felt covered in blood, with the skull caved in. In the ambulance, I thought, Dear God, this is the end. The word "death" raced across my mind. But for some reason, I didn't lose my composure. I even thought, What a shame! I just needed one more month to finish my manuscript.

How strange! Having had all that fear about death my whole life, I was facing this final moment as if I'd transcended everything. But surprisingly, it turned out I didn't have serious brain damage, only surface wounds. Of course, the hospitalization that followed was a time of often unbearable hardship and discomfort, but I was fortunate enough to leave there alive and well. Just like that, I was brought back to life once again. Counting these two near-death experiences, I could say I've been practically reborn, a mere nine-year-old now.

Reader, I've always felt death lingering nearby. Sometimes I wanted to take flight out of fear. But none of us will ever outsmart this destiny or be completely free from our fear of death. Only when I accepted this unchangeable fact was I able to change my relationship with life. Every day is now a surprising gift, and it still astounds me that I've survived all those close calls. Now, near the end of my life, I finally understand—because the shadow of death was always looming so close by, my life burned brighter.

Some may mistake me for being some kind of master Taoist, enlightened enough to feel no fear in the face of death. But what kind of human would be so enlightened? Sure, I now appreciate the role of death in sweetening this dear, dear life, but still, the prospect of death is as terrifying and unfamiliar as it feels sickeningly real. It's just that I try my best to live my life without letting myself get fixated on it, because it's not in my power to change this human fate. Every morning, after the elation on another day, follows the thought of death without fail. Even so, I tuck it away into a far corner of my mind, thinking, "Well, here's to another day—let's get started and have some fun!" And with this positive mindset, I can keep death at bay during the day. Thankfully so.

When I was a little kid, elderly relatives on my mother's side had a custom-made casket in one corner of their traditional Korean living room, and would lie in it day and night. It was a ritual for them to embrace the approaching death.

How do we ever overcome something like death? We can't. We just try our best not to let our fear overrun us completely. All we can do is train ourselves to humbly accept this fate. If you continue to resist and resent death, you will always be frustrated with your powerlessness and end up hurting your loved ones as well. In old age, when you have to get your affairs in order and enjoy peaceful last days, you might instead wind up torturing yourself, enraged at the world and spiteful to other people. You would not only put yourself in so much undue pain, but also leave indelible scars on the hearts of your loved ones who would have to let you go, one way or another.

Make Peace with the Inevitable Guest

Death is the name of the most important guest you'll have to greet in your life. My reader, every one of us must prepare thoroughly to welcome this guest, little by little, day by day. And there's no better farewell present for your loved ones than your natural and peaceful embracing of death. So I make sure to practice for the day this guest will eventually arrive on my doorstep, expected yet unannounced. May the day come in peace, and may my family cherish their fond memories of me once I'm gone.

2

BE GRATEFUL TO YOUR
LIFE PARTNER

"I WON'T" AND "I can't" both signify rejection. But they're different in nuance. You say "I can't" when your rejection is supported
by clearly laid-out reasons: "I can't *because* . . ." Because of this,
the rejected don't take it personally, even though the reasons
themselves could be highly subjective and personal. But "I won't"
is based on your personal feelings of resistance, and therefore
tends to come across as much more biased. You "won't" do
something because, essentially, you just don't feel like it.

We all have the universal desire to be accepted by others,
to be loved. So anyone would feel the fear of "being disliked"
and "being rejected." That's why rejection is challenging to both
parties, whether rejecting or rejected. You can also unexpect-
edly hurt each other in the process of rejection.

This is not to say that you should become a pushover
and never say no to anyone. Not being able to say no, even
when you definitely should, leads to a whole different set of
problems. My point is, in order to foster a healthy relationship,
you should also learn how to reject well, and hone your skills.
So I've always emphasized the importance of switching from
"no" to "I can't because." "I can't," which implies some reasoning,

puts less emphasis on rejection, and allows the rejected to take the rejection with a grain of salt, depending on the why.

But like the Korean saying "Even a monk cannot shave his own head"(중이 제 머리 못 깎는다), it turned out I haven't set the best example of my own long-defended advice. One day it occurred to me that I don't use a variety of expressions with my wife and resort to "I don't want to," "I don't know," or "No." I only recognized this speech pattern of mine when my daughter told me out of nowhere, "You're really chatty today, so unlike you!" We were in a car on our way to a fancy dinner, my treat. My son-in-law chimed in, "It might be because your mother's not here today, honey."

That's when I realized that my response to my wife was usually limited to negative statements without much elaboration. With my patients and students, I've always emphasized the importance of not resorting to this kind of language with their partners, and I've never liked this rhetoric myself, but to my wife I'd been repeating "no" day and night. What a fool! How on earth did I end up like this?

As we grew older and I started to feel my wife bringing up what I considered to be petty things, I've become partial to this rhetoric of "no." Even when she worried about my health, I brushed it off as nagging and just blocked her out. I would think, "Oh, this subject again," and would not reply or engage. When my feelings got hurt, I'd spit like a rebellious teenage boy, "I don't want to."

After all, I wasn't so different from the numerous couples who constantly bickered with each other and came to me for marriage counseling. They all said, "My spouse will never change. We've been fighting over this same thing our whole marriage," or "My spouse was just born this way. Can't change. I'm the idiot here—to think I'm still in this marriage!" They all put their spouses in boxes. They believed they knew their spouses best, found fault with everything they did, and refused to listen when their spouses tried to initiate a conversation, quick to expect just the same old, same old. And these biases slowly built a gulf, a great space between the two of them that became harder and harder to cross. I've observed too many times how a couple who have stellar reputations outside their household come home to nasty, full-blown fights every day, all because of these biases.

It's a common trap in an older relationship—to put your partner in a box. With time, the world changes and so do people, but your perception of your partner does not always keep up. Naturally, you become less inquisitive and more indifferent. Even your fights settle into the same pattern. And once all this accrued tension reaches a breaking point, you might even start to think about separating. It's a real shame—when two people, who each had a rose-tinted vision of the other and lived in a fantasy world together at the beginning of their relationship, grow exhausted and eventually turn on each other.

If you're getting tired of fights with your partner, you should ask yourself if you've also put your partner in a box. Your biased perception of them must have formed over a long time, so it can't be changed overnight. In order to change it, you need to make conscious efforts, and I recommend the following three steps.

First, listen to and wait for your partner to finish the sentence. Whenever a couple comes for marriage or relationship counseling, I always assign them this homework of taking turns to talk. When one person's doing the talking, the other must listen. Otherwise, they'll end up cutting each other off mid-sentence and going red in the face with a rising temper.

One of the major reasons that you fall into the same fighting pattern is your emotional reaction. Even though every fight starts differently, they all tend to unearth those old grudges of yours, and of course, leave you blaming each other. Even if your partner seems to unfairly criticize you in fights, don't let your anger take over, and listen first. Keep your emotions in check. Your partner will become much more open to conversation after letting off some steam. Only then does the real fight begin. When we lead with our emotions, fights become a regular occurrence, but if we are able to approach them with a level-headed attitude, there's a way out of even the worst of them.

Second, don't try to analyze too much. When there's a conflict or issue between you and your partner, you might try to overanalyze the root of the problem. But believe me, that approach rarely ever resolves the conflict or issue itself. This "I know you best" attitude is most often observed in those who like to scrutinise and criticize their partners, count their wrongs, and demand them to change, and these people are quick to blame their partners, which gets them nowhere.

But how much of another person can you really understand, no matter how long you might have been together? After all, we Koreans say, "You can plumb the water ten fathoms deep, but never someone's mind" (열 길 물속은 알아도 한 길 사람 속은 모른다). We're all biased and can only study others from our own perspective. Whoever you think your partner is, in truth, is nothing more than your own interpretation or projection. That's why you shouldn't try to hastily label or tailor your partner to your liking.

And even if you were right on some accounts, what can possibly be done? People don't change easily. Genetics, family relationships, and social circumstances all play into a person's personality, which becomes, in turn, inseparable from the path of life that person's taken so far. How would you be able to change that personality, formed over decades, overnight? And what a great tragedy it is, if you, nonetheless, spend ten or twenty years trying to change your partner and you both end up resenting each other.

Your partner is someone you need to accept, rather than comprehensively understand. Think about this—wasn't one of the reasons you decided to get married in the first place the sure presence of someone who'd always be on your side? Didn't you want from marriage someone who would accept you the way you are? Accept your partner, likewise, before you think to complain your partner won't change. If you continue to stick with your biased perspective, remain critical, and refuse to accept your partner, you'll always end up creating more conflicts.

Third, choose better rhetoric. From the beginning of our marriage, my wife and I had a rule that we would take a moment and switch to honorifics when on the verge of a fight. Honorifics have always been highly effective in allowing us to calm down and take a step back, before re-examining what's going on. And of course, it's not exactly easy to resort to profanity when the other person's using honorifics. In Korean, honorifics also extend to verb changes, leading to a drastic shift in speech and setting the tone for the conversation to follow. While they differ in form, most languages have honorifics that allow you to express utmost respect for the other person, and I recommend using that polite form of speech when you find yourself on the verge of a fight. This method also helps you recover your self-esteem, which might have taken some hits from all the fights, and can make you respect each other.

When I realized how I'd been treating my wife, I immediately applied these three of my own prescriptions to my marriage. One, I listened to my wife, no matter what. Two, I accepted her for who she was. And three, instead of a curt "no," I would say "I can't, because . . ." and articulated my reasons, in response to those concerned questions I'd been seeing as "nagging." At these simple changes in my rhetoric, my wife gave me a quick look and then stopped herself too. What couldn't be stopped with all my expressions of resistance was so simply solved by my respectful language. Such is the tricky nature of marriage, my reader.

I look back on all the years I've spent with my wife. A cheeky girl, intelligent college student, strong mother of four, respected sociologist, and white-haired grandma—all these colorful stories are bound as one on my wife's face. If one woman's life can be so versatile, how can I ever assume I know my wife so well? In old age, your partner is your best friend. Before you lose that irreplaceable friend, consider whether or not you too have allowed your clouded judgment to put them in a box.

3

EMBRACE THE JOY OF
KNOWING LESS

A FEW MONTHS AGO, the café where I've been a regular for the last three years went out of business. It was a cozy, beautiful café where the owner worked alone, without any other staff. As if to complete its comfy ambience, its shelves show-cased knitted objects and coffee cups made by the owner herself, a testament to her good taste. I'd feel right at home as soon as I took a seat there. It was my favorite place for casual appoint-ments, and when a program at Family Academia let out, I'd often join a throng of members going for tea or coffee at this café.

The owner opened the café upon her return to Korea after having lived overseas for a long time, but she decided to move away again, hence the permanent closure of her café. She said she was deeply sorry to close the café and let down her loyal regulars. But there was something poking at my conscience. Never once in the last three years had I bothered to pay the café's name any mind! Everyone called it "the white café on the hill," so I had no incentive to learn the name by heart, I sup-pose. I hesitantly asked her: "I'm sorry, but could you tell me a bit about the name of your café?"

"It's Casa de Gina. 'Casa' means 'house' in Spanish, and Gina is my Spanish name."

I felt a faint sense of regret at not having cared to ask earlier. After a short silence, the owner asked me, as if she'd always been curious too.

"Why do you always order a cappuccino?"

I have a confession to make—I know nothing about coffee. For about three decades, from my first job to my retirement, I only drank instant coffee. But gradually, I started to see coffee of various origins and brands on the shelves, and cafés with menus of more than twenty kinds of coffee sprouting up— all of which was enough to make me dizzy. No caffeinated beverage connoisseur, I opted for cappuccino simply for its cinnamon-dusted top, and even now, it's my usual go-to.

I said: "In primary school, I used to be classmates with the son of an Eastern herbalist, who liked to bring a fistful of cinnamon to school and share it with the class every day. It was a time of Japanese colonial rule, when we all lived in poverty. So imagine what a treat it was to us all. It was the only snack we got. And what an unforgettable taste."

Having said that, I found it absurd that I learned the name of the café I'd frequented for three years only at the time of its permanent closing, and that I didn't know anything about this poison of my choice—cappuccino—except for its pairing with cinnamon powder. Compelled to do better, back home I looked up the origin of cappuccino. "Cappuccino," it turned out, originated in the Franciscan Order of Friars Minor Capuchin in Italy. The friars of this order had a hood, called *cappuccio* in Italian, attached to their uniform, and cappuccino was named after this hood because the beverage's frothy brown top resembled the hood.

I finally know the café's name, its meaning, and the origin of cappuccino, but my favorite café would no longer be there. After all, they say you recognize youthful love only in retrospect—that you don't know what you've got until it's gone.

I guess some things in life don't always align as they should; we're one beat too late at times.

Life's always been that way, hasn't it? The kind of wisdom I could have used in times of crisis was always gained further down the road. I only got the hang of parenting when my children were all grown up. My wife's hair had already turned snow white when I finally learned how to express my gratitude for her. Now that I'm as old as my mother was when she passed away, I at long last understand the physical and emotional duress she must have been under in her old age. I feel the familiar sentiment: "If only I knew then what I know now." Wouldn't that have lightened this load of unbearable regrets and remorse?

But I sometimes wonder, too—if I could go back fifty years into the past, would I be able to make better choices, or lead a better life? After much thought, I always end up shaking my head, no. More knowledge doesn't mean a better life. In all fairness, my ignorance sometimes allowed me to be brave, and because I had no place in the world, I kept fighting. Since I had no sight of so much hurt ahead, I could dive headlong into the thick of life, and because I wasn't aware of failures awaiting, I took on challenge after challenge. If I knew how things would turn out well in advance, could I have been so reckless, persistent, and full of life? Wouldn't I have spent my days resigned and depressed, afraid of trying my hand at anything?

What makes humans powerful? I think it is hope—that tomorrow will be better than today. This hope keeps us alive. And hope stems from "not knowing." We know today, but not tomorrow. So we strive to lead tomorrow in a better direction. This kind of hope keeps us fighting despair and anger. Don't underestimate the power of not knowing, my reader. We have all tried so hard because we didn't know what the future held, and so here we are, living our present.

Embrace the Joy of Knowing Less

In old age, many people tend to feel down and resigned as if they know everything there is to know now. They complain that there will be nothing new going forward, that the future won't have many surprises in store for them. But no matter how old we are, we're always new to the very stage of life we're going through at the moment. I might be eighty-seven this year, but I have never lived the life of an eighty-seven-year-old before. Which is to say, I'm no different from anyone much younger when it comes to my ignorance of that mysterious continent called tomorrow. So, as long as you're breathing, I encourage you to stay inquisitive. Don't be afraid of trying out new things and taking on a challenge, however small, however big. That's the only way for us humans to live, ignorant as we are of our own future.

Even so, one day, you might still end up having a fit of regret and repeating the old mantra "If only I knew it then," but when you do, don't forget that's an echo bounced off of the life you've lived as well as you possibly could. And remember, my reader, for better or worse, even if you had known it then, it might not have changed a single thing.

4

IT'S A SMALL, SMALL WORLD

How many acquaintances do 7 billion people—our entire global population—each need in order to find themselves socially connected? This intriguing question was posed by an American psychologist, Stanley Milgram. In 1967, he tested how many exclusive acquaintances it takes for two strangers in separate regions to end up socially connected, in what we now call the small-world experiment. As it turns out, we need six acquaintances on average. To exaggerate, this means that the entire world is befriended, in a sense, when everyone's got at least six acquaintances each.

In our age of high-speed internet, this theory still holds up. In 2008, Microsoft analyzed messenger chats and came up with a statistical observation that each user was, on average, just 6.6 social connections away from any other. In 2016, Facebook studies found that these connections could even be as few as three. Either way, it's clear that we're living in a world far smaller than we might think.

I've had quite a few opportunities to see what a small world we're living in. I don't have my own car, so I often take a cab, and for some reason I seem to keep running into unexpected people when I do. One time, a cab driver who looked about my age asked me if I was from Daegu by any chance. He probably picked up on the echoes of my Daegu dialect. I told him I was indeed born and grew up in Daegu, and he asked:

"Do you happen to know *so-and-so*?"

Of course, I did. This so-and-so was a thug who was notorious in my hometown back when I was a student. He was known for his swift feet and being like a dog with a bone, and word on the street said even gangsters from another town had never once defeated him in a fight.

"Of course—the whole of Daegu knows him. I myself actually took a beating from him in an alley once."

In middle school, I was tall for my age, which made me an easy target for thugs in my neighborhood. I even learned karate after having been randomly beaten like that quite a few times.

"Oh my god, you have no idea how sorry I am. I'm that so-and-so. It was all terrible foolishness in youth. I turned my life around and am making an honest living now."

What a coincidence! A chuckle escaped my mouth—I thought I'd never see him again in my life, but a twist of fate planted me in the car of this thug who had beaten me up so badly! When it was time for me to pay for my ride and get off, he refused to take my money, repeating his apology. He drove away after telling me it took such a weight off his shoulders to have run into me and finally been able to apologize. He sure seemed just as quick to make an exit as in the old days.

Let me share this story of another bizarre small-world encounter in a cab. Once I hailed a cab near Gwanghwamun to get to Dongdaemun, and a young cab driver blurted, "Sir, are you heading for the Ewha Hospital, by chance?"

How on earth did he know? I sat entirely clueless until the driver finally explained: he was a soldier who had received medical treatments from me when I was an army doctor, after which he safely returned to his platoon. We had quite the chat about the good old days during the ride. At Dongdaemun, where I was getting off, he also refused to take my money. But I thrust in his hands a few bills more than my fare and ran away before he could say a word more in protest.

Consider this for a moment: what do you think might have happened had I mistreated him in my army days because he was just one of many patients? What if I'd wronged him somehow? Don't you think this story could have been in an entirely different genre? One that could send a chill down your spine? So how fortunate that I hadn't, and that our serendipitous reunion was mutually enjoyable? Again, I realized the importance of not mistreating anyone passing through my life.

Gapjil (갑질) is such a hot potato in South Korea these days. It refers to the abusive actions of a topdog, anyone in the position of power—*gap* in Korean—toward an underdog. Extreme cases even involve acts of physical and verbal violence. Why do some people mistreat and look down on others? It's probably because they see other people as a means to an end. Means and tools are easy to dispose of and replace when you can't bend them to your will.

This kind of instrumentalization of humans is prevalent in our society. It doesn't stop at just *gapjil*; its full scope extends to the harsh evaluation of the younger generations based solely on their résumés, mass layoffs without warning, sexual assaults happening all around the country, and customers' abuse of call-center employees; this all falls within the range of dangerously fading humanity. These problems arise when one fails to see other people as equals, as human beings.

Even if our society's been turning a blind eye to these issues until now, it's time that we all contemplated how to recover our collective humanity, kindness toward each other. Why drive ourselves into a hellish match of rankings and keep comparing our wallets, when the truly pressing issue today is of making our society a liveable place for everyone? Not forgetting manners is the least we can do for each other.

Anyone who knows me knows I'm extremely partial to the Korean word *inyeon* (인연). It means the connections that bind us—the human relationship. Just as Milgram discovered in the small-world experiment, human relationships are like an interweaving of tendrils. Through this web of social entanglements, we influence each other. You never know how the consequences of your actions will catch up with you. How would I ever have known that one day I'd get into a cab driven by the thug who'd beaten me up forty years earlier? How could the thug have known? If you remember this simple truth of *inyeon*, of the interconnectedness of all human relationships, you won't think to be unkind to anyone in your life.

A Korean saying says that "Even a petty rock that meets the toe of your shoe is a work of fate" (길에 돌도 연분이 있어야 찬다). If a petty rock that stops at your foot is a fateful connection, what about human relationships? Be kind to those who come into your life. Remember—this world is a small, small place. Your acts of unkindness won't be just written off.

5

WE'RE ALL IN THIS TOGETHER

"WHEN I LOOK BACK on my life, I realize I've met so many good people," a senior professor of mine once said during a lecture for our Family Academia members. He didn't mean that he had been intentionally selective about the people he'd let into his life; he simply happened to have encountered a lot of good people over the years. He modestly referred to himself as a lucky guy. But of course, I knew that it was his amiable personality and his warm, generous smile that attracted these good-natured connections.

No one stands alone in this world. The bowl of steamed rice you wolf down without much thought has passed through so many hands to reach your table—how many more so for a person's life? Parents, teachers, friends, and countless others who have crossed my path have shaped me into the person I am today. When I consider how interconnected we all are, I realize that I am undoubtedly indebted to everyone. This is why I can't stress enough the importance of sharing what we have and giving back to the community.

I started volunteering in Nepal in 1989, initially driven by my love for mountains. I had always fantasized about the Himalayas. When I visited Nepal for the first time in 1982, I quickly became fascinated by the spiritual nature of Nepalese culture. I learned so much from my time in Nepal and kept thinking about what I could possibly do to repay all these generous favors. Naturally, my expertise was in medicine. Hence, I started the Ewha Medical Volunteer Group, as I mentioned in an earlier chapter, and for thirteen years I traveled to Nepal every winter break to provide free medical services to patients in remote Nepalese regions, until I retired in 2011.

Another pillar of my commitment to volunteering is my sponsorship of the Gwangmyeong Orphanage. The initial connection was actually made by my mother, who was known for her compassionate heart. She took care of war orphans entrusted to the orphanage by refugees fleeing to Daegu during the Korean War. Coincidentally, I was later stationed nearby as an army doctor, and since then, I've been volunteering at the orphanage.

I particularly wanted to do everything I could, as a doctor, to reach out to these children with broken hearts and help them heal. That's how the idea of establishing the Muha Cultural Sarangbang (무하문화사랑방)[4] was born, with the aim of offering the kids art activities and educational programs.

Some people commend me for my long-standing commitment to volunteering. However, it wasn't exactly my plan, so I typically respond to these kind words by saying that it just happened that way. I simply loved Nepal, and the only significant contribution I could make was with my medical knowledge and skills. For the war orphans, I thought the best thing I could do was help them heal their broken hearts through art, and I happened to know many poets and artists who could assist, as I've always been an avid follower of the art world. I merely helped put these different puzzle pieces together. I did what I could, time and time again, without ever intending to make a grand plan or lifetime commitment as a volunteer. So these words of praise I often receive genuinely humble me.

Indeed, I believe that everyone should learn to share. However, I don't believe that what we share needs to be substantial. You don't need to carve out a huge amount of time for volunteering or donate a large sum of money. Sharing doesn't have to be that difficult. You might put off donating until you're financially secure and earning more than you currently do. But money isn't the only thing you can share. If you think hard enough, you can undoubtedly find something you can share and come up with other ways to give back to your community.

One day, I took a taxi, and the driver asked me how old I was. I was feeling rather playful, so I told him my birth year instead, 1935. After crunching the numbers in a moment's silence, the driver said, "You don't look your age! You look great, sir!" I chuckled inside. Looking great—with all of my health conditions? Of course, the driver couldn't have meant it; he was trying to make me feel good about myself. I was touched by this kind gesture, and replied, "Thank you for saying that."

During my ride, the driver shared stories about his late father. When it was time for me to get off and I handed him my credit card, the driver shook his head and said: "My father passed away at eighty-one. I wish I'd treated him better when he was alive. So, as a rule, I don't charge any customer over eighty-one." How touching—to honor his father by being kind to the elderly. He had certainly thought up his own wonderful way to share what he could.

Another story about a taxi ride. This was from the time when I was teaching a course in a graduate program at Korea University. This time, I got into a taxi near Ewha University Hospital. The driver, who looked very young, asked me where I was heading.

"To Korea University."

"Oh, you're heading into campus? Please tell me which building, and I'll take you straight to the door."

How kind! The driver navigated the campus effortlessly and stopped at my destination. I handed him the fare, which he refused to take. It turned out this driver was a student at the university himself, and he said he couldn't possibly charge a professor teaching at his school. He was working part-time to save some money for tuition during the break. Again, I was deeply moved by the generosity of this young man who practiced the virtue of sharing even as a working student, so I thrust more than my fare into his hand and ran away.

Buddhists propose that there are seven non-material gifts, referred to as *mujaechilshi* (무재칠시 / 無財七施). These include a tender and comforting gaze, a face that beams with a compassionate smile, polite and beautiful words, kind actions, a gentle and understanding heart, the generosity to offer comfortable seats to others, and the kindness to provide someone with a place to sleep. Reflect on this, dear reader. Was it not the smallest act of kindness that always took you by surprise and moved you so? Offer to others what you seek in them.

Do not overthink it, but start small. Volunteering is not different from any other activity. The truth is, you don't need great wealth or an abundance of time to give back to your community. You can find something to share from what you have, and there is always something you can do. The path to a life of meaningful sharing begins with recognizing those small acts of kindness you can afford to do right this second.

6

LIVE SIMPLY, AND SIMPLER

LET ME BE HONEST—I was born an only son into a wealthy family. In my early life I wanted for nothing. Probably owing to this, I'm still ignorant and somewhat indifferent when it comes to finances. As far back as I can remember, money has held no real power over me. By power I mean the kind that can destroy or send me over the moon. When my family business eventually went under and my father subsequently passed away, things were so bad that we didn't know what we were going to have for the next meal. But my mother told me—a high school student at the time—just to focus on my studies. And so I remained clueless when it came to money, even though my family was in a dire financial situation.

When I was in college our landlord used to lug bags of junk all the way from the US army base, lay out everything in the front yard, and sort out and sell anything reusable. Anyone who stepped in through our front gate could smell the trash, and flies swarmed our house. My sister was so ashamed that she hardly ever brought any of her friends home. But I didn't think much of it and invited even the girls I was studying with. That's how little I was concerned with notions of money, or poverty for that matter. That's probably why I had the nerve to ask my wife to marry me back then. I was up to my neck in debt, but I quite recklessly assumed that I'd get through it somehow.

For our honeymoon years, my wife and I rented a small room in the house of a bank's branch manager in Yongdu-dong, and went on to have our first child there. As my son started to totter on his own, he took to playing in the front yard. One day, he drew a line across the front yard and told me that no one should cross that line to the other side. I asked him why, to which he answered that the other side belongs to the owner of the house. To worry about house ownership at such a young age! My heart ached for him—what a sorry father I was that day.

Even so, funnily enough, I never thought to make more money to provide my son with a better house. Instead, I thought of ways to make things better for him with what we already had. I couldn't afford those fancy toys or an expensive stroller. So I came up with an idea. I plastered the walls and floor of our room with sheets of paper, and on this blank canvas I drew a house, mountains, a bicycle, me, my wife, and the people my son met regularly, each marked with its name. Then I varnished the drawing so it would last for a long time. While my wife and I were away at work, my son played with his babysitter, reading names from the drawings, and when we returned home, he would recite all the words he'd learned during the day.

When I look back, yes, I see it was a time of poverty when I didn't know what tomorrow held for us. But I was also more creative with what little means I had. I mean, the world of toys I got to know as a grandparent was like nothing I've ever imagined. My granddaughter had an entire set of toy kitchenware for playing house—virtually an entire kitchenette—and I couldn't have told my grandson's toy car from the real one if it wasn't for the size. But these polished toys also seemed to provide too rigid a framework for children's playtime. Does anyone else sometimes wonder if, perhaps, the old-fashioned playtime with nothing but a sandbox with some flowers and plants might have been better for children's creativity?

Money can be an easy solution to many problems, sure, but it also limits your freedom in more than one way. I have an acquaintance who used to be wealthy but went bankrupt and lost everything during South Korea's IMF crisis. A lot of our mutual friends stepped in to help and set him up with job interviews, but he always turned down the offer with the same answer—he couldn't possibly work that kind of job. He meant that he, a former business owner who used to have a hundred employees working for him, refused to work "beneath his station." I wondered if his experience of great wealth came to limit his perspective on life, so much so that he became entirely closed to the world he wasn't used to.

We all agree that money's important, don't we? The longer we live, the truer this may be. A life of financial dependence is miserable. We should all learn to make a living ourselves. And our sense of dignity and self-esteem is deeply rooted in our financial independence. So, naturally, you have to make a wise financial plan for your postretirement life. Not everyone will end up a millionaire, but it'd be the responsible thing to plan out our future finances well before retirement.

However, as important as money is, we tend to worry way too much about it. Many people, regardless of their savings, live with this nagging sense that something might go wrong and they won't have enough. They live with a constant thirst for money, so to speak. This psychological state is so prevalent today that the British psychologist Roger Henderson even named it MSS (Money Sickness Syndrome). This term refers to the condition in which you worry obsessively about money even when you're financially secure.

So what makes us worry? Usually, the root cause of all fears and worries is one and the same: our ignorance. Because we don't fully understand what to expect in old age, we're afraid to grow old, and because we never know what comes after death, we're afraid of death. Likewise, because we don't know how much money we'll actually need in the future (or for a rainy day), we get worried and obsessed over matters of money. Some say a solid retirement plan requires 1 billion Korean won, others 2 billion Korean won, but those are very rough estimates. If you want to golf, go on trips, and lead a fancy lifestyle, even 2 billion might not suffice. But do you really need all that? What do you need money for? Exactly how much money, not a dime more or less, do you actually *need*? You can always quit golf, and you don't have to travel around. When you think for yourself, not for the world, you learn to find pragmatic, detailed answers to all these questions money throws at you. You may even overcome your worry and fear about money. You will find in yourself the bravery to make do with little.

In old age, savings of course are something you can bank on, but you also need to become your own seasoned book-keeper. Money's always a means, never an end. Remember—we control and make use of the money, not the other way around. Sure, why not grab all the money while you can—but don't forget to play it like a fiddle and make it work for you.

One great virtue you can foster is the courage to live on little, if you need to. Until her very last day on earth, my mother was very frugal. She made side dishes with seasonal mountain herbs and sewed up old clothes herself rather than throwing them away. She didn't let money get in her way even when she had little to her name, and found her sense of purpose at the Buddhist temples. With or without money, she lived a happy life. And that's about the healthiest relationship with money

I've ever seen anyone have. Money exists for our freedom, but we must not compromise our freedom for the sake of money. Don't be afraid of living simply, or simpler. Learning to embrace a simple life can set you free in old age.

I certainly aspire for a simple life myself. One of my oldest to-dos is to have my room cleaned out like a monk's. Which is to say, to have a minimalist life. I dream of living the simple life of bare minimums and absolute essentials. And I want to invest all else in doing the kind of work that I find meaningful and engaging. As the German psychologist Erich Fromm said, I aspire for the "life of existence not possession."

In reality, my room brims with all kinds of trinkets. Books tower over me and the floor's often littered with sheets of paper. I try my best to clean up after myself, but it is what it is. What can be done? I want fewer material things crowding my room, and a far simpler life. But there's no way to go about this other than more frequent cleaning and the constant practice of letting go, a nuisance though it might be. If I don't learn to let go soon enough, my children will find it even harder to let go of my things once I'm gone, won't they? For the sake of my remaining days, for the sake of my children after I'm gone, I'd better throw out the things that no longer inspire a spark of joy in me.

In old age, simplicity is your best friend. This is as true for your financial choices and your lifestyle as it is for your emotions and inner world. When older, you might find yourself emotionally contrived and disorganized, and probably have a lot on your mind. Even if you don't have a medical condition, old age can slow down your thinking and get in the way of your associative abilities. What's worse, memory problems can leave you feeling scatterbrained. If you've ever experienced it yourself or witnessed someone struggling to get to the point or going off track way too often, it's all symptoms of that compromised thinking ability.

It's the same way with emotion. Since strong feelings are followed by physical, visceral reactions, any extreme emotional escalation in old age can cause aberrations in health, even life-threatening ones.

I have a cautionary tale to share with you about a colleague of mine who passed away the night after attending his best friend's funeral. Unlike other guests, he couldn't stop heaving with tears in front of his friend's funeral photo. Everyone tried to calm him down, but he was unable to contain himself. Shortly after he got back home from the funeral, he passed away out of the blue. He had a few health conditions, but none of them were serious. His overwhelming grief was the cause of his death.

Overwhelming joy can also put you in danger in old age. Back in 2009, I was overtaken with such joy during my volunteer trip to Nepal. The student who had joined me on my very first trip to Nepal was again joining me that year, now as a professor, and with a group of his own students. I was exhilarated that the little seed of good intention I'd planted two decades ago was finally coming to full fruition, and wanted to shout, for all to hear, from the rooftops. It wasn't plain joy, either, but I felt what was so close to elation, or even ecstasy. With such extreme feelings overtaking my body, however, my blood pressure shot up. I took all the medicines I could find to stop it, and tried to relax, but for the whole week I spent on the Nepalese frontier, my blood pressure kept rising and rising, and only stabilized once I returned to Kathmandu.

In old age, you should keep in check all of *he-noh-ae-rak* (희노애락: the four essential emotions—joy, anger, sorrow, and pleasure), so that not a single one peaks out of control. In old age, your sensory organs are dulled, and yes, there's an upside to this relative numbness since it might protect you from extreme emotions. Even so, you should learn to keep your emotions in check. I do not mean that you should suppress or ignore feelings that are already there. That kind of control will only cause the bottled-up feelings to explode further down the line. A good example would be *hwa-byung* (화병: illness of anger), a psychological condition observed in many Asian people of older generations who have been forced to suppress their anger for a long time. What I mean is, you must refrain from those behavioral patterns I mentioned: reading too much into things or blowing things out of proportion. Instead, learn to take everything as it comes, simply, so that your emotional muscle, just like your cardiac muscle, can grow stronger with practice.

The older you get, the more set in your ways you become—and the quicker you are to react to stimuli in these set ways, which might make the muscle-strengthening exercise complicated. It might prove to be a long-winded road. The easiest exercise, I suggest, is to try and acknowledge your feelings for what they are before they build up. In short, if you're getting angry, express that emotion verbally by saying "I'm angry," and if you're feeling upset, say "I'm upset." One of the primary reasons why bottled-up feelings explode is because you haven't vented in a timely manner. You bottle up little moments, which will accumulate and explode somewhere down the road. And you might even feel, in such a moment, entitled to an unreasonable degree of sympathy from other people. But how would anyone understand what you haven't verbally expressed? A healthy relationship starts with the safe space you create for each other to open up and share what and how you feel. So be generous with verbal expression of your feelings. That's the first step to training your emotional muscles.

The next is to find the perfect word for what you're feeling. Whenever you're seething with anger, you don't just feel pure anger. Under the surface might be sadness and self-pity over having been wronged somehow. If you search for and develop a wide vocabulary for your feelings, you learn to avoid getting fixated on one dominant element in the complex concoction of your feelings and falsely amplify that alone. What's more, the process of articulating how you feel might itself prove cathartic.

I once had an elderly female patient seeking help for her marriage problems. She often experienced her chest tightening and rage burbling up her throat, symptoms of *hwa-byung* (화병) from years of unresolved emotional conflicts with her husband. She deplored her forty years of married life with a selfish man who put her through unimaginable hardship. I could tell it would have indeed required superhuman patience to put up with him for so long. I asked her if she'd ever told her husband, "I cannot go on like this anymore" or "Things have to change." She said she'd never even tried. Her entire life, she'd just held her tongue, swallowing complaints. I asked her to bring her husband along sometime. But she never did, and she never sat down to have a heart-to-heart with him either. It took her longer and longer to come back for counseling, and soon she stopped altogether. I couldn't help feeling disheartened. If you just suppress strong feelings and do nothing about them, you really don't know how they might explode one day. Even if that patient never resorted to drastic measures, she'd still have had those unresolved feelings on her deathbed. To not be free of emotional baggage even on your deathbed—what a burden, and what a shame!

In old age, people often feel it's time to get things in order—to let go of old grudges and make up with people you're not on good terms with. However put, it's a simple wish for a chance to leave this world with a lightened heart. If you want to feel that freedom on your last day on earth, you have to start paving a road to that destination sooner rather than later. Just as you need to rid your home of excess clutter to make it nice and tidy, you need to air out your heart to reach a state of emotional simplicity. And there's no better way to get there than learning how to accept and express your feelings. If you become an expert in reading and communicating your emotions, you're going to be in the clear, my reader. Don't forget these two secrets, if you also wish for the bliss of simplicity.

7

PERSEVERANCE

BACK IN 2011, I was sorting through my phonebook and came across the number of my second cousin. I called him and he picked up right away, answering in a gleeful voice. I asked after him, to which he replied, "Cousin, I'm in a nursing home!"

"Oh, you're volunteering?"

He had been an avid volunteer after his retirement as a Korean literature teacher, so much so that he made it quite a few times into local newspapers in Gangneung. So naturally, I assumed he was volunteering again. My cousin explained, "No, I meant I'm *in* a nursing home now. I guess it's time that I volunteered for myself."

"Goodness, your wife must be going through a hard time!"

"Well, she's with me here. I've got Parkinson's, and my wife can't really walk with her bad joints, so here we are."

"Quite the honeymoon, I see."

I was saddened by the news of their illnesses but also felt relief at the fact that they were in the nursing home together, at the very least. It'd be a blessing for both you and your spouse to have lifetimes of health before passing on the exact same day, but that's not really in our power, is it? In old age, a lot of people have to deal with grieving after the passing of their spouses, on top of their own illnesses. So I'd say it's good for your mental health to have your spouse by your side, regardless of your health conditions.

⌇

"PROFESSOR RHEE, MY WIFE died today."

One day, I got this text out of nowhere from my former senior professor. I was taken aback. Both the professor and his wife were pushing ninety, so I really shouldn't have been so surprised, no matter how much I wished them well. But I didn't expect his wife—much healthier than the professor, who'd always had a lot of health problems—to pass before him. How would he handle everything without his wife, who had been his best supporter and caretaker? I was not alone in these worries about him, and a lot of our mutual acquaintances felt the same.

At the funeral, he looked like he'd shrunk in size overnight. Of course, he must have felt as if half of his own body had been ripped apart, having lost his life companion and best advocate. When he saw me, he broke into a wail and vented that he was so torn, and didn't even know if he should just follow his wife or hang on to life still. I couldn't possibly fathom the depths of his grief. After a long silence, I finally told him, in the hope of changing his mind:

"Confucius said human life is the affair of heaven. None of us chose to be born, sir. And none of us opted for the fate of death at birth. But it's not in our power to change that, nor do we have a say in this human destiny. I wish that you'll cherish life until the day heaven calls you up."

A few days later, he texted me: "Professor Rhee, I do want to hang on till I'm ninety, at least."

Eighty-eight at the time, he was saying he'd like two more years to live. But I don't think he necessarily meant he wished for exactly two more years on earth. I believe that he wanted to convey his determination, despite his great loss, to keep on till the very end. And probably a bit of human vulnerability, his waning courage in the face of what had happened. I told him that I believe in him, and that he would be able to face all this head-on. I sincerely hoped I could make him feel better.

"Perseverance." The dictionary defines the word as "persistence in doing something despite difficulty or delay in achieving success." In a wrestling match, there's a position called par terre. It's a French word that means to crouch down on the ground, and accordingly, the wrestler—as a penalty—has to crouch down on the ground and handle the attacks from behind. If the wrestler manages to last long enough, the penalty lifts, and the wrestler is allowed to stand back up and fight again. Truth be told, perseverance is a virtue required most often of those who are already down. For it means to face a situation that's completely out of our control and yet find a way to keep going.

Life is made of ups and downs, so there will be times when you feel your life sails on smoothly like a brand-new convertible on a highway, or times when you stumble upon hurdles after more hurdles, like a tractor trying to make its way along a muddy, unpaved road in the country. There will be times when you feel invincible, and times when you find yourself in the gutter and want to give up on everything. Each life surely comes with its share of drawbacks, but after each rough patch, you'll be rewarded with better years. So perseverance is one of the most important virtues for us humans. How do you cope with a storm, other than seeking refuge in the comfort of your safe abode and waiting for it to pass? It's the same for life—you keep a low profile when things get tough and wait them out.

In the grand scheme of things, all humans will have no choice but to persevere at some points. Every one of us, in truth, is weak, not strong; a loser, not a winner. Because none of us will be able to evade the inevitable ending—death. Someday, we'll all get weak in body and mind, and have to leave all of our worldly possessions behind. This is the same even for those of us who manage to reach the highest esteem, accumulate great wealth, or collect stellar accomplishments to their names. So, some people become cynical, incorrigible nihilists. They ask, "Why try when all this will be for nothing?"

These people have made a mistake in understanding perseverance as a passive attitude to life. Yes, I agree that life can feel like an endless stretch that requires exhausting perseverance, with so many things out of our control unravelling one after another. We're dragged on by the scruff of the neck and pushed around by fate. And this kind of helpless passivity, of course, infuriates us, and justifiably so. It's in our human nature to want to make our own decisions in life, and when forced to face the fact that life is a passive obedience to fate, who wouldn't feel frustrated and infuriated?

I'd say, on the one hand, they're right on many accounts. Some say life is free for us to create, but many life-deciding factors are given and decided for you from the very start. Factors such as your nationality, sex, and family tend to determine the major directions of your life. So, to a large extent, life is a so-called destiny, and once born, we're bound to obey our destiny. No one can help it.

But even though we might not be able to change our destiny itself, we can choose how to handle it. This is one of the ways we become navigators of our own lives. Active involvement with life starts from this place of acceptance. Even when your destiny itself is a given, once you embrace it as your own, you learn to love your life and find happiness within its parameters. The reason we're still deeply moved by stories of seemingly impossible human victories is not because those victors could completely change their own destiny, but because of how they handled what life threw at them. The most inspiring life, then, perhaps is one of both painful self-awareness and unwavering perseverance in the face of our reality. Just like my former senior professor, who decided to face life head-on, even so close to ninety.

It's so easy to hold fate accountable, especially when things aren't going your way, isn't it? You know, go ahead and blame it all on fate. You've done your best, so go easy on yourself. I get it. But then, once you've gathered yourself, keep your chin up and start over. It is also our fate to play this unwinnable game, no matter how many times we lose. We must all learn, my reader, to get used to this nasty thing called fate. We have been born, if not of our own volition, born and alive nonetheless. And it is your life, not anyone else's, so why not give it all you've got, just because? Life you haven't fully owned will always come back to haunt you someday and become the worst kind of regret on your deathbed. At the end of the day lived to the fullest awaits a sweet, good night's rest, and my reader, at the end of a life lived to the fullest awaits peaceful death. To those who lived their lives to the fullest (진인사 / 盡人事), heaven will finally answer for their wait (대천명 / 待天命). Such is the truth of Confucius's famous words.

8

Never Underestimate the Power of Ordinary Happiness

A FRIEND OF MINE'S got an exceptional memory. When we start chatting, all the memories I have pushed to the back of my mind suddenly come flooding back in a vivid surge. The hilarious predicaments we found ourselves in while intoxicated; that one time I took the fall for a friend's transgression; or the chance encounter with a poet we admired at a café, where we spontaneously started an informal conference of sorts—the list goes on and on. During our conversations, I always find myself envying my friend for having such a rich cornucopia of memories inside his head. After all, the more heartwarming memories you have, the better equipped you are to handle the potentially lonely and challenging days of old age.

While at my office desk, I often find myself reminiscing over a cup of tea. Not that my mind dwells on special memories like life-altering trips or accomplishments or honors; most of the time, I find myself thinking about the sort of ordinary moments that everyone has. Like the good times I've had with my children, pleasant conversations with my patients, or the sense of peace I've felt on hiking trips. And those ordinary memories, even before I know it, bring a smile to my lips, my heart swelling with the warmth of deep joy and filling me with the strength to tackle another day head on.

One of my happiest memories to this day remains the year when my wife was abroad on sabbatical as part of the foreign exchange program for professors and I got to spend more time with my children. Fortunately, we had an aide to help take care of stuff around the house, and a friend of my wife's agreed to drop off and pick up my kids, so I could juggle my job at the hospital and the task of looking after my children. But on the weekends, I was completely lost as to how to keep my four kids—all in elementary school—entertained. At the time, one of South Korea's biggest newspapers, the *Hankook Ilbo*, happened to be hosting a weekly event, "The Weekend Tortoise Marathon," and I signed us up, spending every subsequent Sunday for a year running alongside my children.

The marathon route started and ended at the National Theater of Korea in Jangchung-dong, with the Namsan Octagonal Pavilion serving as the halfway point. And true to its namesake, the Tortoise Marathon didn't goad participants into sprinting or competing for first place, and instead celebrated the beauty of galloping or strolling at one's own pace. So my family resorted to taking a long walk together, playful and leisurely, in step with each other. To this day, I can't say I've seen anything more beautiful in my life than my children on those Sundays, glistening with sweat in the warm sun and causing quite the ruckus up the stairs to the pavilion.

After a short break at the pavilion, we would return to the theater for a prize draw. We would sit in a little huddle on the staircase and wait until the last name was called out loud. For the entire year, we'd wait for one of our names to be announced, always in vain. But anticipation itself was still a little joy we always cherished. After yet another prize draw that won us nothing, we would go to a Hamhung-style cold buck-wheat noodle place in Ojang-dong before going back home.

These ordinary moments I got to spend with my children remain the happiest memories in my life. Even now, I think of the marathon when I pass by the pavilion, when I come across young parents walking with their children hand in hand, or when I see my children playing with my grandchildren. And whenever I do, I make a silent wish that they will cherish their moments too, and that they will have more in years to come. After all, these ordinary, everyday moments are the key ingredients in the recipe for a happy life.

Now that I've reached this stage in my life, about 80 percent of the time when my friends and I meet up and sit around, we talk about our past. Interestingly enough, my friends, like me, also bring up the most ordinary memories, the mundanity of everyday life, with such fondness. It's uncanny. In my youth, I was driven by the pursuit of happiness and security, which seemed so tantalizingly out of reach, but as I'm nearing the twilight of my life, I see that happiness has always been nearby, and I could indeed grasp it whenever I wanted to. But what can be done now? Happiness in itself is a rare luxury you get to enjoy only from time to time in our repetitive daily life. I'm not saying that ordinary happiness should be the objective of your life. Happiness, of course, comes to you as a natural course of events when you live your life to the fullest.

I'm just saying that you need to keep an eye out for the pockets of happiness hidden in your everyday life. Tomorrow, you'll probably find yourself in a traffic jam, overworking, disagreeing with your superior, fatigued from looking after your children, and falling asleep with a smartphone in your hand, again. Your daily routine itself is inevitable. Then why not look on the bright side, and try to look for the small joys in the everyday? You may find observing your fellow passengers enlightening fun, make your morning more enjoyable by sharing a cup of coffee with your coworker, or make a game out of cooking and doing the dishes with your child. If you can't avoid something, at least don't let it ruin your mood. That's the key to maintaining a positive outlook on life and creating as many cherished memories as possible.

Some people like to comment on my so-called "optimism" and even envy me for it. But who's to say one person is purely optimistic or pessimistic? There are always two sides to everyone's perspective on life. It's probably just that people interpret as optimism the flexibility with which I accept things in life. But there's only one secret to my so-called optimism, my reader. It's just my sheer determination to look on the bright side and find joy under any or all unavoidable circumstances.

I start my day with the mindset that I'll find and store away another pleasing memory today that I can bank on in the future when I might not be able to move on my own. This mindset allows me to uncover many possibilities of happiness within reach.

I'm happy to wake up to another day, and to get to enjoy yet another morning in my life. I'm happy to be able to watch a show on TV, as my hearing and health are still good enough. I'm happy to be able to perform an easy task on my computer, despite my partial blindness. I'm happy about the prospect of going out for a cab ride around the Skyway.

Such small, ordinary yet precious moments as these may just become the glorious, glimmering backdrop of your life one day. A day's worth of good memories someday may lend you the strength to carry on. So, my dear reader, remember to keep an eye out for good memories you can make right here, right now. We can find happiness in all of the most unexpected corners of our everyday life.

9

LIFE IS A STORY YOU SHOULD READ
TILL THE VERY LAST PAGE

"YOU'VE SAID NOTHING WRONG but . . ."

That's what my father-in-law used to say when I was young. I was one opinionated young man. I had a clear sense of good and bad, right and wrong, and like and dislike. So I fumed over the wrongs and fought to correct them. I always spoke my mind. My father-in-law never finished the sentence, worried as he was. He must have known. I was too hot-blooded and too young to understand the way of the world, even if he'd tried to tell me.

I came to learn, little by little, year after year, what he must have meant by such an elusive remark. There's no absolute good or evil in this world, where evil lurks in good, and good emerges out of evil. What good intentions start often ends with bad outcomes, and what looks bad at first can turn out to be a blessing in disguise. Every coin has two sides, and we find out how the story ends only when it does end.

My life came with a fair share of dark turns. But were they truly crises? When I look back, I realize in every moment of a crisis I found a new door opening. No, it may be that my desperate attempts to hang on always led to new opportunities. Every time I thought it was a dead end, I always found a small side road leading me somewhere new. There's no true dead end in life, my reader, except for death. So you can't see the true picture of a life that hasn't come to an end yet.

As a young man, I was an aspiring artist who liked poetry and visual art, and of course wanted to major in arts. But having taken care of my ill parents, I decided to become a doctor. Once I got into med school, however, I found it hard to catch up on all the studying. I just couldn't get into anatomy, physiology, or pathology, all of which was a lot to a literature nerd like myself. And all the energy I'd been suppressing at home with my overprotective mother brought me to a boiling point in college. My long-repressed frustration and rebellious spirit at its peak, it was virtually impossible for me to just sit and study. I unleashed all this pent-up energy by running a hiking club. I went hiking on Jiri Mountain for days on end, got holed up in a forge to make crampons as I'd read about in a book, and even once found myself stranded on a snowy mountain for three days. But one of these detours, hiking, became my lifelong passion afterward. While I was having a hard time at med school, I found the spiritual companions of my life—mountains.

As I shared with you, reader, earlier in the book, when I was busy working as a resident doctor, I got arrested for my role in the April Revolution and found myself in prison. When it happened, it was as if the sky folded in on me. Why punish me for something I did back in college, all those years ago? I was a newlywed, and hoping to open an office of my own once I became a specialized doctor, but out of the blue, I got this life-crushing sentence. Once released, I was completely lost. With my record, I couldn't apply to study abroad, and no one would hire me. After many sleepless nights, I wrote to the head of a national psychiatric asylum that most Korean doctors avoided, in hopes that at least there might be an open position. Thankfully I got the job.

It was my last resort: the only door that I could open at the time. But during my time there, I grew as a medical practitioner in a way I wouldn't have done elsewhere. I participated in many national-level projects, networked with esteemed doctors from across the country, and gained a lot of firsthand experience. Had I worked at a university hospital, I would have had a couple of mentors and only come across patients with a small range of known conditions. Because I worked at a stigmatized federal institution, I was ironically granted the enriching experience of meeting with a variety of doctors and patients. I'd go so far as to say that my criminal record was a blessing in disguise for my career as a medical practitioner.

Once I settled in, I thought life was done messing around with me. But out of nowhere, I was ordered to serve in the military. The story is, when the April Revolution was re-evaluated, my criminal record was stricken clean, as were all the other incarcerated demonstrators'. Now that I had the chance to pursue my dream in medicine, however, I received a letter of notification demanding three years of mandatory military service which I'd been exempt from because of my record. I was finally thinking about opening my own clinic, having got some experience, when again, I had to put my life on hold for three whole years.

At the end of my military service, I was right back where I'd started. I had no savings left to finance my own clinic, but didn't wish to go back to the asylum either. I met up with more established doctors in my field and asked them for advice on my career. Back then, there were not many psychiatrists in Korea, so I could actually meet with most of them. When I visited Yonsei University Severance Hospital to introduce myself, the chief there asked me what I wanted to do for the rest of my career. For the first time, I confessed that I wanted to teach, but since it looked out of reach, I was debating opening my own clinic.

I'd always been a studious kid. If I had something on my mind, I had this tendency to try and get to the bottom of it. I could see I'd be more of an asset and feel at home in academia, which allowed time and space to deliberate, rather than a huge medical institute inundated with various tasks that called for always thinking on your feet. But I missed my chance to pursue that path when I was sent to prison, so I thought professorship just wasn't in my life's book.

To my surprise, however, a few days after my visit, the chief called me to offer a full-time instructor position. Another unexpected new door. I spent the next three years teaching and studying hard. The national asylum gave me firsthand experience in my field, and Yonsei University Severance Hospital gave me the time to rediscover and cultivate my scholarly side. Afterward, I found a permanent position at Ewha University Hospital and spent the rest of my life as a teaching doctor.

As you'll know by this point, dear reader, my life didn't go as planned. Whenever I tried to do something, I met a hurdle or had my wings clipped. Sometimes I lamented why on earth all this happened to just me. But if I were not to give up, I needed to do something, anything. And always, my struggle to hold on to a last straw earned me a new chance in the end. A new door leading to an entirely different world that I had never even considered before.

So this is why we should never make haste to conclude we know life inside out. This world may not be as it seems, after all. What you think is the end, my reader, might not be an end at all. If you just hang in there, you'll most likely find a way out. Life is a story you should read till the very last page. No one ever knows what the world has in store for you.

Even at eighty-seven, I don't think I understand much about the world. My hometown was a battlefield. I feared I'd die in the war before I even got to grow old. In college, I dreamed of democracy, but was pessimistic in the face of the government's atrocities. In my middle age, I was sick of people's materialistic views but didn't think another lifestyle would be possible in my country that was fixated on economic growth and nothing else. But look at South Korea now—a thriving democratic country where everyone has a smartphone in their hand, freely communicates with the rest of the globe, aspires to a good work–life balance, and dreams of living true to oneself. Eighty-seven years ago, I wouldn't have imagined the world would look like this.

Taoists say that one epiphany is only a stepping stone to another. When you think you know everything there is to know, you fail to see other possibilities you haven't yet considered. You lock yourself up in your own little world. Never assume what you know is all there is to reality. If you keep on believing in second chances when everything seems to have ended, you will find a new door opening somewhere in that dead end. This is the only truth I know of life and can share with you, my reader, with absolute confidence, having lived eighty-seven years.

Translator's Note

B Y THE TIME I first met Rhee in person, years before translating this book, he and my mother had been writing to each other for sometime. Their correspondence started because someone in our family has a neurodiverse background and required regular help from mental health facilities. Rhee is one of the few trailblazers who tremendously improved the conditions of South Korea's mental health system, and we happen to be one of many families indebted to his hard work over the last few decades.

Even before his work as a psychiatrist touched the lives of many neurodiverse patients and their families in South Korea, he had participated in key democratic movements and, as a result, had to sacrifice a big part of his twenties as an incarcerated activist. For the last few years I've known him personally, however, what I've found most consistently astounding about him is his down-to-earth, honest, and deeply genuine personality.

As a member of the younger Korean generation, I've found it hard to connect with the older generations on a deep level. But I also find Rhee's generation fascinating, because they have lived through the unimaginable, from the war and era-defining activist movements to financial, political, and cultural crises of my homeland. They're arguably the most traumatized Korean generation today, and probably the least expressive about their shared traumas.

Rhee's book is one—the first one, indeed—that allowed me to truly connect with a voice from his generation, that offered timeless insights on life that did not lack in knowledge and expertise, life experience, or empathy. He doesn't use his voice to harshly chide and mindlessly pamper his readers, or to glorify a dogma. While translating, I found solace in that lack of overzealousness. Some self-help and inspirational books today—especially those available in English—urge their readers to overachieve and goad them like personal trainers, not only in dealing with life's setbacks and personal issues but also in decompressing and finding their true paths in life. Rhee's book, instead, lays things out as he sees them, coming from a deeply personal place. Yes, that's the place from which he says, calmly and simply, "life [is] driven by the forces of great coincidence and many chance encounters." And I imagine that's a place someone like him, after living through so much and for so many meaningful missions, can reach near the end of one's life.

His voice is such a salve, which I didn't expect from someone who's seen the worst of his country, personally and historically. Despite all that he's been through, Rhee still finds much to be grateful for in his life and wakes up excited every day. Only after retirement in his seventies did he become a bestselling writer. And now that he's pushing ninety, another long dream of his is coming true: his English debut as a writer. And this is a journey I believe many English readers will find as inspiring as I have.

As the original Korean text was in a freeform style, due in part to the context-driven nature of the source language and Korean readers' familiarity with a fluid rhythm, Rhee and I worked to give the English edition a more accessible structure. This book is a result of many thoughtful hours spent moving around, retitling and regrouping its chapters to make the book sing and each section more cohesive. It would not have been possible without Rhee's generosity to allow for as much creative license in translation as he could provide and wonderful insights from our editor at Rider, Suzanne. My gratitude also extends to our improvised dream team in South Korea, Rhee's assistant and his wife, Lee, who both handled countless emails back and forth and did not let one thing go amiss despite Rhee's vision impairment; and Rhee's grandson, who stepped in as a second reader on his behalf when the first draft of the English edition was ready.

It's no exaggeration when I say it's a great personal and professional honor to be part of this journey as his translator. Many of my generation remain indebted to people like Rhee who fought to make their homelands free, democratic, and more just and socially aware. But I go about my days blissfully forgetful most of the time, much thanks to those who worked to afford us this relative peace. In Rhee's own words, in our interconnected global community today, we influence each other's lives to greater extents than we might imagine. My hope is that, with this book, I've done my part in amplifying his voice for you, reader, and connecting his world and yours.

NOTES

1 Michel de Montaigne, *That to Study Philosophy Is to Learn to Die* (1580).
2 Shin Young Bok, <감옥으로부터의 사색> | *Thoughts from Behind Bars* (돌베개, 1998).
3 Anthony Storr, *Solitude: A Return to the Self* (Free Press: 1998).
4 *Muha* (무하) is Rhee's *ho*—an official name a person of quality from older Korean generations received, usually from esteemed scholars or public or literary figures; *sarangbang* refers to a specific part of the traditional Korean house, *hanok*, where the male head of the family resides and entertains important guests.